Yola,

Mixed Feelings

Lis McDermott

Best wishes

Lis & Conrad-

WORDCATCHER publishing

Mixed Feelings
A True Story
Wordcatcher Real Life and True Stories

Published in the UK by Wordcatcher Publishing
www.wordcatcher.com
facebook.com/WordcatcherPublishing
@WordcatcherCom

First Edition: October 2018

Paperback ISBN: 9781912056545
Ebook ISBN: 9781911265238

Category: Autobiography

For our parents,
Florence and William, Irene, and Eddie
and all our friends who have supported us
along the way.

2017

The old lady stopped in her tracks and stared from one to the other. A good look at him; a good look at her and back again. They may as well have been aliens judging from the effect they had on her…

Contents

1950s –
World News

- 1950 world population: 2.556 billion
- Queen Elizabeth II succeeds to the throne, 1952; coronation, 1953
- Edmund Hilary and Tenzing Norgay reach the summit of Mount Everest, 1953
- Double-helix structure of DNA discovered, 1953
- First James Bond novel by Ian Fleming, *Casino Royale,* published, 1953
- Roger Bannister runs the sub-4-minute mile, 1954
- First children receive the polio vaccine, 1954
- Ruth Ellis is the last woman to be hung, 1955
- Rosa Parks refuses to sit in the back of a bus, breaking the segregated seating law in Alabama, USA, 1955
- Felix Wankel (Germany) develops rotary internal combustion engine, 1956
- Hard disk drive invented by IBM, 1956
- First Russian earth-orbiting satellite *Sputnik* launched, 1957
- Race riots in Notting Hill, 1958

UK Prime Ministers

Clement Attlee, 1945-51
Winston Churchill, 1951-55
Anthony Eden, 1955-57
Harold Macmillan, 1957-63

1950s – Lis

I was plucked from my mother's womb on 8th March, 1952, probably to fit in with the doctor's schedule. Having a caesarean birth at the time my mother was pregnant, I don't suppose she had a lot of choice about the time I made my way into the world. I was born into a Britain that was still living in post-war conditions. This meant that there continued to be food rationing and many cities had large bombsites, showing evidence of the bombing raids of the Second World War, (which had ended in 1945).

Although a huge number of people lived in rented accommodation, my family were lucky enough to own their own house. My mother's father, William Campbell had invested in having a house built in Birstall, a suburb of Leicester.

My parents, Irene and Edwin Ward, were married in June, 1948, after which Dad moved into the home that Mum shared with her disabled brother Ken and her widowed, elderly mother, Elizabeth. Both Mum and Dad had grown up in the same area, although from very different backgrounds. Dad's family lived in a two-up-two-down, with the toilet outside, and Mum's in a house where they were the only residents in the street to have a bathroom. She was particularly proud of this.

Another huge difference between them was their education. Mum went to a private girls' school and Dad to the local boys' school.

I wasn't a particularly sickly baby, but I was lactose intolerant, which meant I spent a lot of time regurgitating my milk onto any outfit Mum was wearing. This must have annoyed her intensely because she loved her clothes. The other thing that surprises me about Mum is how she coped with a new baby, complete with all of the wetness, stickiness, and smells. She was incredibly fussy. She had a nose like a bloodhound and I can imagine when she had to change nappies she probably had a peg on her nose. Then there was the dribbling; she probably spotted drool at 100 yards before it had even had time to develop past a little bit of spittle!

Even when I was older she would never drink out of the same cup as me or share the food we were eating. She certainly wasn't one of those mums who test the baby's food before each mouthful, and had she done that, the spoon would have been washed each time. So, how she coped with those aspects of having a baby, I don't know. What I do know was that she and Dad had been desperate to have a baby. I had arrived and they named me... Lisbeth.

Almost a month before I made my entrance into the world, Princess Elizabeth had a great change forced upon her. She succeeded to the throne at the age of twenty-six when her father, King George VI, died. That is a young age to have such responsibility thrust upon you. Although Dad would always stand for the National Anthem, my parents weren't big Royalists and there was no royal memorabilia around the house.

Whether or not there was any influence from these historical events, I ended up with a name similar to that of the new Queen's. Why, why, why? Not, Elizabeth, Lisa, Liza, Libby, or Elspeth, but… Lisbeth. And not even a middle name that I could use instead. Mum liked a singer called Lizabeth Scott and favoured her name. But, somehow, I ended up with Lisbeth.

This has caused problems throughout my life. When I joined Miss Johnson's class in junior school, she was writing our names up on the board. She kept writing Elizabeth Ward, so I put my hand up to tell her that wasn't right. She wasn't amused and ignored me, saying, "Don't be stupid child, you can't have been christened that."

I tried again, several times. In the end I was sent to the Headmistress. I returned with a note saying that in fact, yes, I did know what I had been christened. Of course, I got no apology. I wonder how she would cope these days with all the different names teachers have to deal with?

Even now, when I sign my signature, helpful secretaries in officialdom seem to think I don't know how to spell my own name and add a 'Z' or an 'E'.

I now know that it is a Scandinavian name, although we have no links there. It remains a mystery as to where Mum found it.

I don't like using my full name, I much prefer the shortened 'Lis', mainly because saying my full name reminds me of Mum telling me off! Despite that, I'm quietly pleased to have a name that is unusual, at least in the UK.

I was told that at around the age of three years old, when tired, my left eye turned inwards. Consequently, I was marched off to the opticians. When we got there, they had the obligatory letter recognition board in the corner of the room. The optician assumed I wouldn't know my letters. However, I did. He started the test and was surprised when I confidently said, "E for Daddy." Mum pointed out that Daddy was called Eddie. The prognosis was that I had a lazy left eye. Therefore, for most of the time growing up I wore glasses, the ugliest possible; round, pink frames, National Health glasses.

During my time at infant school I had periods when my right eye was covered. The idea was to strengthen the lazy left eye but, in reality, it made no difference whatsoever. All that happened was I ended up walking into things and at school I couldn't read anything written on the board or see to write anything. To start with, the eye-cover was on my glasses, but as I used to peep round them the decision was made to have the cover stuck to the skin around my eye. Dad took a great deal of care removing them, but I remember now how painful it was.

Even more disastrous than having my eye covered were the eye drops I was given the day before visiting the opticians. The drops made my vision so blurry that I could see absolutely nothing at all. Never mind what was written on the board, I could barely see the board.

Measles was a common, highly infectious childhood disease in the 1950s and could have serious, lasting effects for some children. When I was ill with this, Mum kept the curtains shut because bright light seemed to cause me problems. I remember being confined to bed, in the dark, and feeling very sorry for myself.

Doctor Gilbert was our family doctor. Although he seemed old to me, he was probably quite young and not long qualified. I don't think he had children himself, otherwise he possibly wouldn't have done what he did.

I loved drawing even then and was sketching a picture of my bear, which someone had lovingly knitted for me. His body, a yellow rectangle with arms and legs, had black embroidered eyes, nose and mouth. His ears were black triangles that blended into the yellow of the body, placed at the top corners of his head. Unlike conventional ears, they didn't stick out from the body. It was when I was drawing the bear that Dr Gilbert dropped in to see how I was recovering.

He took one look at the drawing and said, "He hasn't any ears."

Before I could say anything, he proceeded to draw human ears on the sides of my bear's head. Now my bear had two sets of ears. I wasn't impressed. I was three and a half, going on four, and no, I was no Picasso, but it was my drawing. He should have known better, you don't draw on someone else's work of art!

Holidays were usually spent with another family. Eric and Pat also had an only child, Bill. He was about four years older than me and called me 'Lizzy-Fish'. He is the only person to ever give me this name, thank goodness.

We used to stay in East Runton, near Cromer, in what I can only describe as a wooden cabin. Outside, there was a wooden windmill on a tall pole, like the ones you often see in American wild-west towns. There was a long climb down the cliff face via wooden steps to the windy beach below. Dad didn't like the heat, so he preferred the Eastern coastline around here because of its bracing climate. This meant that it was often chilly, even on sunny days, and sitting on the beach we had to have a windbreak around us to keep warm. Dad used to take Bill and me paddling in the rock pools and occasionally in the sea, though he often got cramp in his feet. He never swam. In fact, neither of my parents did. He also used to make the most amazing boats in the sand. Boats that you could sit in and pretend you were out at sea sailing on the stormy waves. Bill's dad, Eric, didn't seem to have much patience with children and I don't remember him playing with us at all.

I was a real daddy's girl. He used to read to me and play with me a great deal. Once, when Mum was out somewhere, he took me to see his parents. We didn't have a car and Dad often walked, so he decided I would ride on my tricycle, to which he had attached a rope so that he could pull me when I got tired. He got me all dressed up, in my best dress, warm winter coat, warm shoes, and warm gloves and sat me on the tricycle.

"It's cold, Daddy," I said, feeling a tad chilly around the bottom area. He had only forgotten to put my knickers on!

On bath night, it was Dad who used to bathe me and make sure I didn't drown. The best time, after splashing around, was when he would lift me up to stand on the cork lid of the wooden linen box and we'd sing while he wrapped me in the big towel, making sure I was dry. We sang hymns and old songs, such as *In Dublin's Fair City* and *Little Brown Jug.* Always the same songs, but we sang away at the tops of our voices. When I eventually went to school and we sang 'We plough the fields and scatter' they couldn't work out what I was singing. It turned out I was singing the bass line because that's what he'd taught me.

Before starting school, Mum arranged for me to spend the day at an infant school in Leicester where one of her friends was the head teacher. She was worried that, being an only child, I would be upset leaving her for the first time. Especially as we had spent so much time together.

In the 50s there were no pre-schools where children could gradually get used to leaving their mum. Your first day at school was often the first time ever you were away from her. When the day arrived for my visit, off I went without a care in the world. In the morning we made animals out of clay. Next, we painted, which I loved because I was allowed lots of different colour paints and could create what I wanted on a large piece of paper and it didn't matter if I made a mess. After lunch we were all allotted camp beds where we had an afternoon nap and later the day ended with a story. I went home with some clay to play with and was buzzing about what I'd done. Mum wasn't too happy about the mess the clay made – well, more the mess *I made* with the clay.

On the day I started infant school for real I didn't mind leaving Mum at all. I didn't cry but I do remember my best friend Gillian did... until lunchtime.

My reception teacher was Miss Stone. She had sharp features and short, curly, auburn hair. She was strict, but fair and would comfort you if needed.

On my first day I found out quickly about her strict side when she slapped my leg. We were all sitting near the sandpit, each of us wearing our names on labels hung around our necks. Instead of listening to instructions I was talking to Gillian, thus deserving the clout.

The only thing I ever got into trouble for during my whole school life was talking when I should have been listening. Not a lot has changed!

At my infant school, sadly, we didn't go to sleep in the afternoons, but we did get playtime in the sandpit, painting and music, and the afternoon always ended with a story.

Initially I stayed for school dinners, and Mum used to walk Gillian and I to and from school. They were not something I looked forward to as, like Dad, I was a fussy eater.

The dinning hall was at the far side of the concrete playground. Inside, it was a long dark building that smelled of a mixture of floor polish and stewed cabbage. Trestle tables were set out in rows either side of a central aisle and each table had benches along their sides. The kitchen hatches were to the left as you walked into the hall. These were where the food monitors would collect the food and take them to the teacher who sat at the head of each table to serve everyone.

My favourite pudding was chocolate sponge with custard. However, the custard was always pink which, to me, doesn't go with chocolate. Custard was always served in silver- or gold-coloured metal jugs. One day, as food monitor, and as I was walking back from the hatch carrying the custard, I tripped. The custard jug hit the floor on its base and, in one pink mass, the custard leapt up into the air and fell back again into the jug with a splosh. Not one bit of custard spilled out, it was so solid. There was a lot of laughter, admonishment from the teacher for not watching my feet, and then the jug was on the table ready for the waiting chocolate sponge.

Then there was the 'swede incident'. Miss Barrar was on dinner duty. She was a strict, harsh, teacher who most children were scared of, me included. I had been given swede but didn't eat many vegetables at the time. Dad didn't eat any vegetables apart from frozen peas, so why should I? The swede was making me feel sick. Miss Barrar told me that I couldn't leave the table or have pudding until I'd eaten all the swede on my plate. You didn't argue with

Miss Barrar, so I tried to eat it, but with each mouthful I felt sicker. She told me not to be silly.

So, I threw up.

Mum decided I wasn't going to be bullied into eating things so from then on I went home for lunch. It took me years to eat swede after that, but now I love them and most other vegetables.

As an only child, I spent a lot of time contentedly playing alone. A constant in my life has been an inanimate object that continues to link me back to my childhood; my teddy bear, Ding-a-Ling. My maternal grandmother bought him for me when I was born. For me there is a real emotional connection whenever I see anything about teddy bears. On reflection, I wonder if Ding-a-Ling was in fact a kind of surrogate sibling, as I was always asking my parents if I could have a brother or sister. I love the fact that Grayson Perry (the artist) as an adult still has a love for his teddy bear, Mr Pickles.

Ding-a-Ling got his name because he has a bell inside him that jingles against his hard tummy when he is shaken. Not, as someone suggested, because he was named after Chuck Berry's song, *My Ding-a-Ling*. He isn't a big bear, only 11 inches tall, and he has a rather serious look, but I love him! He has been a loyal bear and has gone on every move with me, including to college. He now sits on my desk watching me while I work, and while I'm writing this.

My friend, Gillian, had a bear called Growler. Not surprisingly he made a growling sound when you bent him forward. When either of us went on holiday, our bears would come too and stay with each other. We even made them sleeping bags for their sleepovers.

Walking to school on a show-and-tell day, I had Ding-a-Ling with me. I dropped him. When I picked him up, he was silent. I was mortified; he'd lost the sound that gave him his name and his identity. I was so upset, but thankfully Gillian saved the day. She thought that his bell must have got stuck so in the next instant she threw him back to the ground, and to my delight his voice returned.

I mentioned earlier I was used to playing alone, but Mum also encouraged me to invite my friends round to play. We had a long garden, so we didn't disturb her or the neighbours too much.

I had a new girl, who had recently moved to my school, round to play. A few days before, I had finished reading *The Children of Cherry Tree Farm* by Enid Blyton, which had been a gift. My friend showed an interest in it, so I gave it to her. When she left, and I was putting things away, Mum asked me where the book was. I told her I'd given it to my friend and she was annoyed. I was confused. Why was she telling me off for something she had always encouraged me to do? I had shared my things, so what was wrong? She was worried about me becoming spoilt and selfish, which I understand, but at the time there were too many mixed messages.

It's strange how, when I look back, summers always appeared to be sunny. I don't remember them being wet or cold like they often are now. I can't imagine that they were always like that, but that's the picture my memory paints.

We used to have happy times with the three of us on holiday when I was little. I remember, when I was about six, we went on holiday to Old Colwyn, Wales. Each day we'd walk down to the beach on a track called The Dingle, which ran under an aqueduct that in those days carried the railway and steam trains along by the seafront. I remember the three of us holding hands and singing *As I was going to Strawberry Fair*, as we walked down the track.

Mum and Dad both sang in choirs. Often when we were at home they had their friends round in the evening and they would play the piano and sing. I'd lie in bed listening. Mum had a lovely voice and it often reduced me to tears.

While in Old Colwyn we visited Llandudno. Throughout the summer holidays there was an outside stage in Happy Valley on the Great Orme. Entertainment was provided for the holidaymakers and during the performance they asked children to go up on stage and perform their party piece. Mum told me to go up and inside I wanted to perform, but my legs wouldn't let me move from the spot. Disappointed, I watched and listened to the other children as they sang or recited poems, with tears streaming down my face. I longed to be up on that stage, but I didn't have the nerve. The feeling from that day of self-sabotage has stayed with me and, on occasion, has reappeared, although I'm overcoming it.

For a short time when I was seven, I went to ballet lessons, mainly because Gillian did. When my teacher wanted me to do exams though I wasn't too keen. I had been nagging Mum about learning the piano. We had one at home and I was always tinkering around on it. I loved the sound of it when Mum played, even though she didn't play well. However, hearing her play gave me a desire to learn. Her reaction to this was that if I learned the piano, when it got to exams I would have to take them, and I would have to stop ballet lessons.

Mr Lawrence Embrey, my piano teacher, lived on the new estate, within walking distance from our house. I loved my first lesson. He had both grand *and* upright pianos in his front room, where he taught. I learned on the grand, which felt so special. The feeling of achievement when I played my first tune while reading music was immense. He marked little arrows on the music pointing to the up and down direction of the tune; even though the tune only had three notes!

My lessons were a mixture of theory, where we'd sit by the open fire and I'd write in a little book, and piano playing. Looking back, I recognise he was a good teacher because he taught the theory and aural alongside the practical playing so I built up my skills in tandem.

The day I got the results of my first exam, Mum was out and by the time she came home I was in bed. Dad had suggested we play a trick on her, so when she came to ask how I'd got on, I was trying to look sad. It worked because she hugged me saying, "Don't worry, love, you can do it again."

She was delighted when I excitedly told her I'd passed with distinction. My career in music had started.

In the summer of 1959 I was excited when I was invited to stay with Aunty Lila and Uncle Harry in Lytham St Annes. Uncle Harry was Mum's distant relation and Aunty Lila was his second wife. I don't think Mum approved of her. Lila dyed her hair blonde and always looked glamorous; definitely the sort of woman you should be suspicious of in my mum's eyes.

St Annes was the destination of previous holidays, so I knew some of the area. Harry and Lila lived in a bungalow that wasn't too far from the sand dunes and sea, which were magic to play in. I did find it strange staying in the bungalow, as I wasn't used to having bedrooms on the same floor as the other rooms.

I had always wanted curly hair and once Mum put curlers in my hair overnight. I woke up because they were hurting, and I couldn't sleep well, so she took them out and showed me my hair in the mirror. I couldn't believe it. I looked just like Eva Anderson, a girl in my class who had beautiful, long, curly hair. I was so happy and couldn't wait to get to school the next day for everyone to see. You can probably guess what happened. My hair is super-fine and all of the curls dropped out, so by the next morning it was as straight as it had always been. I was so disappointed. So, you can imagine, when Aunty Lila asked me if I'd like my hair curling, of course I said yes! She took me to her hairdressers, and they gave me a light perm. I was absolutely delighted. I had curls, just what I'd always wanted.

When I got home after my wonderful visit, Mum wasn't so delighted. She was furious. How dare Lila take it upon herself to get me a perm? I don't think they spoke for some time… but I was happy.

1960s –
World News

- 1960 world population: 3.039 billion
- First working laser built in the US, 1960
- First communications satellite and weather satellite launched, 1960
- Wall built between East and West Berlin, 1961
- John F. Kennedy becomes 35th President of the US, 1961
- Vietnam war begins, 1961
- Russian, Yuri Gagarin, is the first man to orbit the earth, 1961
- Jamaica gains independence, 1962
- First transatlantic TV transmission via Telstar, 1962
- John F. Kennedy assassinated by Lee Harvey Oswald, 1963
- Martin Luther King gives his "I have a dream" speech, 1963
- First commercial nuclear reactor, 1963
- Nelson Mandela sentenced to life imprisonment, 1964
- Death penalty for murder abolished in the UK, 1964
- BBC 2 starts broadcasting, 1964
- Malcolm X killed, 1965
- England beat Germany 4-2 in the World Cup, 1966

- 116 children killed in Aberfan, 1966
- BBC Radio stations 1, 2, 3, and 4 all launched, 1967
- Enoch Powell makes controversial "Rivers of blood" speech, 1968
- Martin Luther King assassinated, 1968
- Robert Kennedy assassinated, 1968
- Woodstock music festival, 1969
- Regular colour TV on BBC 1 and ITV, 1969

UK Prime Ministers

Harold MacMillan, 1957-63
Alec Douglas-Home, 1963-64
Harold Wilson, 1964-70

1960s - Lis

Robert was a loner. Even today I can still picture him with blonde hair, cut in short back and sides. Like me, he was an only child of older parents.

I didn't know him. None of us did, he didn't play with us or mix with us unless he had to. He was thought of as a swot by the rest of us. I don't remember making fun of him, but I may have done. I don't remember being purposefully cruel to him, but I may have been. If I did then it would have been without any malice.

His passion was the stars and his idol was

Patrick Moore, the TV astronomer. All Robert was interested in was the planets and stars. Even though the Russians had won the space race, with Yuri Gagarin being the first man to orbit the earth, it seemed to pass some of us by. I don't even remember watching it on TV, though I think we must have done. For Robert, however, this must have been one of the most exciting of times, yet he didn't appear to have anyone to share his passion with.

One day Robert didn't come to school. We were told in assembly that he had died. My parents told me the real version; he had hung himself with his dressing gown cord on the back of his bedroom door.

As an adult it is more than a tragedy that a child should have felt so lost and out of place that he ended his life at the age of 9. How does a child of that age even contemplate suicide? How must his parents have coped?

As children we didn't understand the impact of his loneliness and how cruel some of us may have been. Robert's actions have always stayed with me, and despite not knowing him, I've never forgotten him.

My last year in junior school, death appeared in my young life yet again. Twice.

Dad's father, John Ward, died. I didn't see a lot of Dad's parents due to Mum not getting on well with her mother-in-law. We lived a bus ride away, but they never came to us and, as we didn't own a car, we couldn't fetch them. I was sad when Grandad died, but not devastated. What I remember most about him was that he always gave wet, sloppy kisses. It was like he licked his lips before kissing you. The other thing was that when I had dinner at their house, he and Dad would always play the same trick on me. When I ate my pudding Grandad would ask, "Who's that coming down the yard?" Stupidly I'd look to see, and when I turned back to my pudding he and Dad had hidden it. I say stupidly, because I fell for it every single time.

Because I was only ten, I wasn't allowed to go to the funeral, but before the service we went to Grandma's. As was the custom for some people then, Grandad was in an open coffin in the front room, the best room. Because it was so rarely used, it was also the coldest room in the house, and so, in retrospect, the best place for a body!

Several times during the morning Grandma asked me if I wanted to see him, and each time before I could answer Mum strongly answered "No!" for me.

Mum and I were in the kitchen washing all the cups and saucers that people drink from on these occasions, when Grandad's sister, Nelly, came out of the front room having seen her brother. Wiping away the tears she said, "Eh, he looks just like on his wedding day."

I was shaking with laughter, because I was thinking how awful he must have looked on his wedding day. Mum thought I was upset and started hugging me. When I explained it wasn't tears but laughter, the two of us had to try hard to suppress our giggles.

Grandma got her way in the end. With the pretence of showing me the flowers people had sent, she took me into the front room and quickly whipped off the cloth covering Grandad's face. He looked like an alabaster version of himself, wearing makeup.

For days afterwards, I thought a lot about the fact that our bodies are merely shells and once we're dead that's it, we're not here anymore. I found it disturbing for a while – the thought of not existing. Since then, I've never wanted to see anyone else I loved dead.

The second person I lost that year was my friend, Steven. He had been born with a hole in his heart and was what adults euphemistically described as 'delicate'. A lot of the other kids at school didn't understand why he didn't join in things. We became friends and I was allowed to go and play at his house because I was gentle with him. The games we played had to be activities where he didn't get too excited and short of breath, so mostly our time was spent drawing, colouring, chatting, and laughing together. We had a lot of fun, but nothing strenuous.

At the end of each school day we'd put our chairs up onto the desks, stand behind them and our teacher, Mr Peatfield, would say a prayer before dismissing us. This particular afternoon, before the prayer, he told us he had some sad news. Steven had died, and he led us in prayer in his memory. I was stunned and, not surprisingly, really upset. As well as being upset I felt guilty too. Maybe I'd been too boisterous when playing with him earlier in the week? Perhaps I'd made him laugh too much? Even as a child we turn someone else's death into a situation about us.

I wasn't upset that he'd died too young and missed out on all the life he had ahead of him, that was way beyond my thinking. I missed him and was going to miss playing with him, and his friendship. The adults explained again how ill he had been, and that he probably wouldn't have lived a long, healthy life. As with Robert, I only knew Steven for a short time but, even now, I can see his face clearly.

During the summer holidays, Gillian spent most of her time at her Grandma's house, which was at the other end of the village, so I rarely saw her, or played with her. Instead I played with the only other children around; boys. There were two brothers who lived three houses down from me, Nicky and Charles. Charles was the youngest and always had to tag along with us, much to our annoyance. The same happened with Phillip and Geoffrey, the latter being the youngest brother. We played cricket in the middle of the road, as there was very little traffic. We sat in Nicky and Charles' dad's car, pretending to drive, and when we got older and had bikes we spent our time riding up and down the road. It amuses me, because I remember thinking, *When I grow up to be a big boy, I'll have a watch.* I was obviously a little confused!

Being a bit of a tomboy when I was younger seems to have impacted on my life. I've always made friends with boys and men and have never had a best girl-friend that I shared every minute with. A girlie night out has also never been first choice for entertainment. However, in later life I have made more female friends.

The 60s was the era when youth culture really began. It was the antithesis of the post-war austerity of the 50s. There was a revolution in clothing, with bright colours, mini-skirts, Twiggy and Mary Quant hair-dos, and, of course, The Beatles. I heard my first Beatles song in 1963, I thought it was four girls singing! I became a fan, although I was a little young to be involved in the pop culture revolution taking place.

This was a time when I made lots of new friends, as I moved first to Stonehill Secondary School and then Longslade Upper School. Luckily, I didn't have to sit the eleven-plus exams because, according to my teachers, I wouldn't have passed. Stonehill was the old, original secondary school building and Longslade was a brand-new school. The two sat on the same campus, and while most of our lessons took place at Stonehill, some classes were taught in the newer classrooms of the upper school.

Gillian, along with several other girls in the area, passed the entrance exams and went to Loughborough Girls' High School. For the first time since starting school we were separated. My parents couldn't afford for me to attend the high school, plus as it had been suggested by my primary school, I probably would have failed the exams. In retrospect I also wouldn't have had access to the creative subjects I needed. My ultimate career path would have been very different.

On one of the occasions when we had lessons in

the new building, my friend Christine and I were in line outside the maths room, when a boy called Stephen approached me.

"My mate wants to know if you'll go out with him," he said.

I asked him to point out his mate. Christine and I both looked over to see his good-looking, blonde mate. We conferred about what I should do. I said yes, because his mate was good-looking and did look nice. So, it was decided that I'd meet Patrick at the cinema that night at 7pm. At this point, I hadn't even spoken to him.

We went to see *Von Ryans Express* starring Frank Sinatra. I was more than a little surprised when I turned up to find that Stephen was there too. He was obviously the back up support in case it all went wrong. My back up support was Dad, as Mum, on my asking to go out, agreed as long as Dad was around in case Patrick didn't turn up. Poor Dad, who was totally against his little girl going out on her first date, walked the dog nearby to ensure I was safe.

On our next date, Stephen and my dad didn't come along. Patrick and I went out on and off throughout school and for a short time when I was at college. Mum was never happy about me going out with him because his family were Catholic. I could never understand why this was a problem, but I think she had the idea that if we married all I'd ever do was have babies. For years, because of her prejudice, I was a little wary of Catholicism but didn't understand why as I'd never attended Mass. I don't know if I expected incantations and prayers, but when I did eventually go to a Catholic church, I wondered what all the fuss had been about.

Mum had never been out of the country, and Dad only to fight in the Second World War, and they were keen for me to travel outside the UK. When the French teacher planned a trip to Paris, Christine and I were the only two from our class to go. We stayed in a *lycée* (school) in the centre of Paris with several other school groups. While there we visited the main tourist attractions, including a visit to the Louvre. I was so excited that I was going to be seeing paintings by famous painters such as Da Vinci and Monet and Manet. Dad had a book that I often looked through full of famous masterpieces and now I was going to see some in the flesh. The Mona Lisa always looked so vibrant and big, but, in reality, it was a disappointment. It's such a small painting and didn't have the impact I expected.

In the winter months Mum often washed me in front of the open fire, because we didn't have central heating, and the bathroom was freezing. The 22nd November 1963, was one of these nights. The TV was on and Mum was watching in between helping me wash. A newsflash came on – US President John F. Kennedy had been shot dead in Dallas. Suddenly Mum went quiet. More than being worried, she was scared. She was convinced that as a direct consequence World War III would start. She had already lived through two wars and knew that the Great World War had started in exactly that way, with an assassination. Due to her reaction, I knew it was serious, but I didn't understand.

1964 - Lis

Despite living in a suburb only a few miles away from Leicester, which had a large Asian population, I didn't know anyone who wasn't English and white. The only time I saw 'coloured people' (as we called anyone who wasn't white at that time), they were working as bus conductors and drivers on the buses or in the city centre.

After the Second World War, when the government had welcomed migrant workers from Commonwealth countries to come to the UK, many men from India and Pakistan had taken up the opportunity, looking for work. In Leicester they had come to work in the textile industry, which was the main employment of the city. They brought over their families, wives, and children. Belgrave was one of the areas where private housing was cheap, and this area became one of many mainly Indian and Pakistani areas around the city. This was also where Dad's office was located. Nearly all of the shops on the Melton Road were Asian food or clothes shops. I don't ever remember Dad passing any comment at all about the situation but, of course, Mum did. I always found it fascinating seeing the women dressed in their beautiful saris. I used to love the journey on the bus into Leicester, when I could sit looking through the window at all these brightly coloured shops and differently-dressed people.

One night the three of us were watching our small, black and white, BBC-only, TV. There was a discussion about Malcolm X's visit to talk at the

Oxford Union Society. The debate on TV was whether or not he should be allowed to talk, and even whether he should be allowed into the country. I couldn't see what the problem was, but there were a lot of mumblings from Mum about him keeping his ideas to his own country. This was the same year that the USA passed the Civil Rights Act of 1964. This ended segregation in public places and banned employment discrimination on the basis of race, colour, religion, gender, or national origin. This had first been proposed by President John F. Kennedy, but was signed into law by his successor, Lyndon B. Johnson. Until this time, and even though segregation in schools had been stopped, there was still much inequality in southern United States.

Although I remember seeing pictures on the news of white policemen, batons raised, chasing black people on the streets, as horrendous as it was, it didn't affect me. For a start it wasn't here in my country, it was far away. Being twelve, I wasn't aware enough to understand how it must have felt to be a minority. I didn't understand anything that was happening with regards to race issues and, like many people at the time, I was contentedly living in my comfortable bubble.

I was more interested in The Beatles' latest song, or collecting their photos to stick on the wall in my den, which was in fact the outside loo! Anyone using the outside loo was watched closely by John, Paul, George, and Ringo. Dad allowed me to stick my pictures up in there rather than onto the wallpaper in my bedroom. I did manage to get one picture in my bedroom. I removed the copy of Turner's *The Fighting Temeraire* from a frame and replaced it with a picture of Paul and Jane Asher although I cut the latter from the picture.

The Beatles' film, *A Hard Day's Night* was released that year, and I went to see it with friends. We were so excited because everyone who had seen it said it was brilliant. At the time, it was something new, to see a pop band as lead players in a film. It has been credited as one of the most influential musical films, inspiring others, including the Monkee's TV series. Some of the girls in the audience screamed during the showing, which was annoying, because I wanted to hear the music (I had a similar problem when I went to see films with boyfriends – I wanted to see the film, I didn't go to spend my time kissing). Luckily it didn't last long, and they soon settled down to enjoy it and sing along with the songs. The film was a great success in both box office terms and, as far as I was concerned, as a fan.

I don't know if it was the same in all schools, but in ours you were either a Beatles or a Rolling Stones fan. You weren't both. If people were both, I don't think they would ever have owned up to it. Stones fans thought they were much cooler than The Beatles, who they saw as, disparagingly, the 'boys next door'. I much preferred The Beatles. I liked their music and harmonies, whereas I didn't like Mick Jagger's voice, and to me The Rolling Stones always looked scruffy.

1964 – Conrad

1964: the year that South Africa sentenced Nelson Mandela, as leader of the anti-apartheid struggle, to life imprisonment for sabotage. The same year that in Smethwick in the West Midlands there was a race-focused election. Over 5,000 immigrants from Asia, Africa and the Caribbean had moved into the West Midlands in the last few years and politicians were reacting to the growing sense of resentment in the area.

One Tory poster said:

> *Face the fact:*
> *If you desire a Coloured for*
> *your neighbour vote Labour.*
> *If you are already burdened with one, vote Tory.*
> *The Conservatives once in Office will bring up to*
> *date the Ministry of repatriation to speed up the*
> *return of home-going and expelled immigrants.*[1]

Into this unequal world, I was born on 28th October, 1964. I was born in Birmingham to a large, lively family and was named after a West Indian Cricketer, Conrad Hunt.

My daddy, Wilfred Augustus was born in 1919 in Borobridge, Clarendon, Jamaica. Wilfred never talked about his family, because, he said he'd had an

---

[1] The Huffington Post, 16th March 2015, *Britain's Racist Election showed, 1964 General Election isn't that dissimilar to 2015's.*

unhappy childhood that had caused him to run away from home at the age of seventeen. He moved to Spanish Town, Jamaica.

Mummy, Florence, was born in Alexandra, St Ann, Jamaica in 1927. She lived somewhere near the mountains until the age of sixteen when she also ran away to Spanish Town because she didn't want to work in the sugarcane fields, and desperately wanted an education.

When the Second World War started, they were respectively twenty-one and fourteen. I don't know if the war had any impact on either of their lives, because neither of them ever spoke of it.

Wilfred and Florence married in the early 50s, by which time they already had their children Cynthia, Fitzroy, Blossom and Annette. In 1955 Wilfred moved from Spanish Town to England, following in the footsteps of the many Caribbeans who had travelled to the UK at the end of the war.

That year, the British government had passed The Nationality Act, a law that allowed Commonwealth citizens the right to move to the 'mother country'.

During this year the first large group of post-war West Indian immigrants sailed to the UK. The boat, HMT Empire Windrush carried 492 passengers from Jamaica to London. The British government wanted to fill shortages in the labour market due to the loss of their men during the war. Many of these Caribbeans were attracted by the idea of better prospects and lives. They were given full rights of entry and settlement in Britain. What may have seemed to them as a land paved with gold was anything but that when they arrived here. Many of them disembarked from the Windrush wearing totally inappropriate clothes for the weather.

Although there were many jobs in the National Health Service, British Rail and other public transport, there was no access to private housing, and many were confronted by racism and prejudice. Many only intended staying in the UK for a few years, and though some returned to the West Indies, the majority remained to settle permanently. This group are often now referred to as the Windrush Generation.

Housing was in short supply due to the ravages of war, so many of the newcomers were housed in an air-raid shelter under Clapham Common. Brixton was the nearest place for work and socialising, and the Mayor there welcomed the new immigrants. Many of the newcomers stayed in London, particularly Brixton, but others found work in different areas of the country.

The government hadn't prepared the British population for the immigrants arriving from the colonies. Sadly, the indigenous population either couldn't, or wouldn't, see how these immigrants had provided help when it was needed and asked for. They also seemed to forget how many of the Commonwealth men and women had fought and died in the war alongside the very people who these immigrants were now coming to replace in the labour shortages we had.

As the aftermath of the war meant housing

shortages continued, there were some clashes with the established white community, and clashes worsened in the late 1950s. Riots erupted in several cities and areas, including Birmingham, Nottingham, and Notting Hill, West London. The 1951 census, however, showed that only 3% of the population had been born overseas and the great majority of the immigrants were white and European.

When Wilfred arrived in the UK, due to all the housing shortages it was hard to find somewhere to stay. There were signs that read: 'No Irish, no blacks and no dogs.'

How the newly-arrived Caribbeans coped I can't imagine, but they would eventually find someone who would rent them rooms, and they would share the bathroom and kitchen facilities. A year later, in 1956, Florence joined him along with Cynthia, their eldest.

They sent for the other three children about two years later, and their other children, Cecil, Vincent, Gilbert, Dawn, and myself, were born in Birmingham. For the children coming over from Jamaica, England must have appeared grey, cold, and dull by comparison.

I don't know what Daddy did for a living, but eventually my parents owned their own house in Cannon Hill Road, Edgbaston, near the cricket ground. Whatever his job, it earned enough for a mortgage. Daddy was good with numbers and I remember him going to work every day wearing a suit and hat, and he drove to work in his own car.

In the same way people had helped them when they arrived in England, Wilfred and Florence did the same for others, and rented out rooms in their home. This meant that the house was always full of people.

Mummy worked in the Queen Elizabeth Hospital as a cleaner. She had set hours, and always made sure she was there to take us to and from school. We always felt safe and knew if anything happened we could run to her. She was our rock and also highly respected in the local Jamaican community.

People often came to her for advice and she was so trusted that she ran a 'pardner' scheme. This is where a group of family members and / or friends set up a savings club. She held the money for the scheme and people came to her when they needed it.

Jamaica had recently gained independence from Great Britain in 1962, but this year they took part in the Summer Olympics in Tokyo for the first time as an independent nation. I'm sure that with that and the birth of a new child, there must have been much celebration in the house on Cannon Hill Road. Although Jamaica didn't win any medals, the family gained a little star.

1965-67 – Lis

During my last year at secondary school when I was thirteen I started going out with Richard, who I met at the local church youth club. He was seventeen and my first proper boyfriend I used to see regularly. Richard was serious about me, but he wasn't pushy in any way physically, considering the age difference. Dad wasn't happy about me going out with boys, and although I didn't hear the conversation, I'm sure Mum explained why I should be allowed out. Many of my friends weren't so lucky and ended up skulking around in the shadows with their illicit boyfriends on the way back from Guides, or other such activities. They also had to create the most elaborate stories as to why they were late home. I have never been a good liar and was grateful that my parents trusted me enough to find my own way in the difficult art of dating. Mum and Dad always encouraged me to invite people in for a cup of tea, and from Richard onwards, all my boyfriends came in for their cuppa.

For my fourteenth birthday, he took me to see the film *Cleopatra* starring Richard Burton and Elizabeth Taylor. My parents, who were pretty amazing in their attitude about me going out with him, told him I had to be home by 10.30pm. Richard, being polite, made sure I was home by that time – which meant that we had to walk out before the end of the film (much to my annoyance).

After we had been going out for nearly a year, Richard kissed me properly, and I finished with him. When he gave me my first French kiss, I thought it was disgusting. I realised I didn't fancy him that much, and only liked him as a friend. Poor guy! He stalked me for several weeks; getting up early in the morning and following me around on my paper round. I'd made up my mind though, that was it, I was not going out with him again. His mother always blamed me because he didn't do well in his exams.

There was a song in the charts by The Mersey Beats, called *Sorrow*, which made reference to long, blonde hair and blue eyes, which I have. Annoyingly, Dad used to sing it to me suggesting that I had caused the sorrow.

Kenneth Tynan, a theatre critic and writer caused a massive uproar in the press when he used the 'F' word when appearing on a late-night BBC satirical show. I clearly heard the word but, as there was no reaction from my parents, I was inwardly relieved, thinking they had missed it. The next morning, however, Mum asked me if I'd heard a rude word on TV. When I said yes, I was interrogated as to how I knew it. I'd heard it at school, the older girls used it, and so I knew exactly what it meant. Mum and her friend at work didn't and had both asked their husbands who had refused to tell them, because 'It's a word you don't use in front of ladies.' They even tried to look it up in a dictionary, with no success; it didn't appear in the larger dictionaries until the mid-60s. Eventually, they found out what it meant. Mum asked me if I'd like her to tell me. No! I didn't want to hear her explanation of what it meant, that would have been far too embarrassing.

In the summer of 1966 I moved to the upper school where I started working on my O-levels in Music, English Language, and English Literature, and Certificates of Secondary Education in Art, Religious Education, Maths, Biology, Geography, Cookery, and French. I was in the top set for English and the bottom set for Maths.

Maths lessons were a bit of nightmare. The

class included the people like me who had problems with maths, and the boys who didn't want to be at school and spent most of their time messing about. Sadly, our teacher couldn't cope with the boys, so instead of us being helped through the quagmire of numbers and equations to make any sense of them, he spent his time trying (and failing) to discipline the 'bad' boys. My parents, well Mum, was so worried about my lack of progress in maths, that they hired a private tutor for me. His prognosis was: I wasn't 'thick' but had a huge block when it came to maths. Part of the block may have been Mum and the fact that she was so good at figures. She would regale the story of her trying to teach me how to count to the day she died. It was inconceivable how I didn't understand anything mathematical, so she tended to lose her patience. Dad kept out of it.

The other subject I hated at school was Physical Education and anything sports-related (I continue to have a love-hate relationship with this). Each year, without any choice, we were made to enter the sports day. I always entered the 100 metres as it was the least difficult thing. Despite that, I managed to come last every single year. It was so embarrassing. I was by far, the slowest. Thank goodness it was only once a year.

As there were only three of us in our house, I had a large double bedroom all to myself. The most exciting thing was that my bedroom was going to get a makeover. I had total choice of wallpaper and colour options. The room had a fireplace in it, which I had always hated, so for part of the makeover a friend of my parents made me a long dressing table top that ran the whole length of the wall. This partly covered the offending fireplace and had a range of drawers and shelves below. To me it was the height of coolness! Looking back it was an extremely amateur attempt at built-in furniture. I chose symmetrical wallpaper in varying colours of dark blue, and then had a burnt-orange bedspread. It looked fab and I was so proud of my room.

Music was a huge part of my life; classical and pop music equally. Saturday mornings were taken up with County Youth Orchestra rehearsals. During the week I went for piano lessons and on Sundays all three of us sang in the church choir. When piano practice and homework was done, I spent a lot of time in my newly-decorated bedroom listening to music: *The Beatles, The Beach Boys, The Who, The Four Tops, The Supremes, Gene Pitney* and *Manfred Mann* amongst many, on my second-hand Dansette record player and my transistor radio.

Alongside this music, I could also be playing my classical records: Swan Lake, Grieg Piano Concerto, Scheherazade or the New World Symphony. For Christmas 1966, my main Christmas present from my parents was two albums: The New World Symphony by Dvorak and The Beatles' *Sgt. Pepper's Lonely Hearts Club Band.* The following summer I sang the songs from the latter for the whole train journey to St Anne's on Sea, where we were going for our summer holiday. I probably drove my parents mad, but they didn't complain.

1968 – Lis

My diary of 1968 refers to two things; boys, and O-level exams. Apart from sitting exams, this was one of the best of times.

It's the only such record I have from my youth, and I only saved it because it is an illustrated diary sent to me by my Australian pen friend, Gwenda.

There are a lot of entries about RE lessons and Kev. Kev had dark hair, cut in a fashionable style and was way too good-looking for me – or so I thought. He was going out with Rhona, who wasn't all that either, and I didn't know what he saw in her. He was a smart boy with a gentle manner and we used to chat regularly on the phone about RE – well that was my excuse.

There were also lots of entries about Glyn. Glyn was another viola player in the youth orchestra. He also had dark hair and eyes; I think you'll see there is a type emerging here.

I used to sit in the orchestra, sometimes sharing a music stand with him, and sometimes sitting behind, but always in viewing distance. This would probably make me a stalker these days but, at sixteen, it seemed normal. However, I was actually going out with John, always referred to as 'Little John', because of his height. John, who was a bit shorter than me, was a blind date, set up by Gillian and her then boyfriend, Russ. John was Russ's friend, and they lived close to each other. He didn't go to our school but attended an all-boys school on the other side of

Leicester, where his family had lived prior to moving to Birstall.

The date was pretty inauspicious apart from the fact that the week before, John had knocked all his front teeth out by cycling into an unlit skip parked in the street. He was amazed it didn't put me off, but he was funny, caring, and we had great fun together. He had a younger brother and sister, so I used to love going round to his house and being involved in a larger family. I think his mum had us married off in her head; in mine, definitely not!

Most of our dates were to the cinema, youth club, or babysitting his younger siblings. John bought us matching identity bracelets, (all the rage at the time), and after having our names engraved on them, we swapped, so we wore each other's. Outside school we were inseparable. Our relationship, which was pretty innocent, involved lots and lots of snogging!

Earlier in the year, I had applied for a Saturday job at Marks & Spencer. I went for an interview, but fell at the first hurdle, the maths hurdle. There were several of us and the lady interviewer asked us all what change we would have from five pounds if the item cost nineteen shillings and sixpence. I was still thinking about it when everyone else had answered. I didn't get the job. In those days there weren't calculators or tills that would work the change out for you; you had to work it out in your head.

In the end it was good that I didn't get the job, because I was moved up into the senior section of the Leicestershire Schools Symphony Orchestra which met every Saturday morning. I now had my Saturday mornings organised but wanted to earn too.

Mum had a friend who owned a small dress boutique in Belgrave, Leicester. Despite my lack of maths skills, and the fact I could only work on Saturday afternoons, she kindly took me on as an assistant. I was in heaven, surrounded by affordable and fashionable clothes. Unsurprisingly my earnings didn't go far, they usually went straight back into the till.

Before getting into the Senior Orchestra I'd played in the Intermediate Orchestra and, at the age of sixteen, was one of the oldest. I played the viola to a standard that would never see me promoted to the seniors. This is where fate dealt me a good hand. The one instrument that the orchestra didn't have was a harp. But somehow the orchestra ended up with seven harps that they bought in Wales. The idea was that they would share them around the county, so that students from different areas could learn to play. Sadly, nobody had checked them for woodworm, and several of them literally fell apart. One of the surviving harps was housed in my school, which was where the orchestral rehearsals took place each Saturday. They wanted someone to learn to play who wasn't a leader of any of the instrumental sections and could also read piano music. This was me – back desk of the violas and working on Grade 7 Piano.

I started learning the harp, and this was my golden ticket into the Senior Orchestra. This is how I ended up at a rehearsal, in front of the British conductor, Norman Del Mar. We were rehearsing *Brigg Fair* by Delius. As I was completely inadequate in managing to play what was in front of me, he asked, "Is it too early in the morning, dear, or always too early?"

Not the most encouraging words, but as my teacher was a violinist who had played the harp while in the army, it wasn't surprising I didn't have any technique.

* * *

On 5th June 1968, the American Kennedy family suffered yet another tragedy. Bobby Kennedy captured people's attention and, even in the UK, we were following news about him. He opposed the Vietnam War and was also a supporter of civil rights, things that we were becoming more aware of. The day he was shot we were on exam leave, so we weren't in school, but the next day we wanted to hear what was happening, so I took my transistor radio to school. Our music teacher let us keep it on for updates during the morning.

We heard later that he had died without regaining consciousness. The BBC showed his last journey as a train took his coffin from New York to Washington with thousands of mourners lining the way to pay their respects. I wrote in my diary that it was 'sad but in a beautiful way'. I didn't have the words to express the feeling of loss for someone who had obviously touched so many people.

I wasn't politically minded but I was becoming more aware of world events, and conscious that people in other countries didn't have lives like mine. I clearly remember watching the news, and seeing the Russian tanks driving through the streets of Prague, and a year later, the student Jan Palach set fire to himself in protest against the Russian invasion. He was twenty-one, only five years older than me. In Vietnam, many of the US soldiers were only three years older than me at nineteen. The references to Wilfred Owen's war poetry, particularly *Anthem for Doomed Youth*, which we had started reading in English, strongly resonated with me.

Some of the sixth form students went to London to see the musical *Hair*, which was causing all sorts of uproar, mainly because of the nude scenes, its anti-war sentiment, and in one scene, the desecration of the US flag as it was set alight on stage.

I was becoming aware of the world outside mine, but I lived a life where I was personally unaffected by events. I needed to get the exam results I required so I could go to music college, and then train to be a teacher.

July and August were celebratory months; I passed my Grade 7 Piano exam and got the 5 O-level passes that I needed to be able to move onto my A-levels. I was on track for my chosen career.

1968 – Conrad

One day, a strange woman came to the house, and what happened next turned my whole world upside down. My parents were upset and angry, and I remember us all standing at the front door, my sister and me clinging onto and hiding behind Mummy's skirts. The strange woman stood at the gate along with the police. She had come to take us away with her, because she was our birth mother.

I don't remember either of us crying, or Mummy or Daddy shouting, I only remember being scared. Confused, and with no understanding of the situation, we were led away by our new mother to live in a rented room in a house a little further down the same street.

It turned out that our birth mother, Cynthia, had left us with her parents when we were about two and three years old. We had spent the first four, formative years of our lives with the man and woman we felt safe and secure with, whom I now know as Grandparents. However, they have been, and always will be, my mummy and daddy so as I continue through this story, I'll refer to them as that. My birth parents I'll refer to by their Christian names.

I have since learned how this all came about. Cynthia was living with her parents and already had my sister, Dawn. When Cynthia became pregnant with me, I think her parents, who were Christian people, were unhappy that she was having another child out of wedlock and wanted her to settle down. It was them who arranged for her to marry my father, Fredrick. I think it was a marriage of convenience and know nothing about how they met, and next to nothing about Fredrick.

All of them; Mummy, Daddy and their children; Cynthia, Fredrick, Dawn, and me lived under the same roof. After two years the marriage fell apart and Cynthia and Fredrick separated. I don't know where Fredrick went, but Cynthia, (who had started training to become a midwife and had the opportunity to continue her studies in Canada), packed up and left.

Neither Dawn nor I remember Cynthia and Fredrick in those early days, our only memories are of Mummy and Daddy.

After Cynthia took us away, which was such a shocking move, I think we were in a daze, and didn't know what was happening. Even now I don't remember details of that day. Once we had left things started to change. After the initial move down the road, we moved from Cannon Hill Road altogether to another rented place near the railway track. I remember it as always cold, and Dawn and I shared a room. At night we used to have a glass bottle filled with hot water and wrapped in a sock to keep us warm, as there were no radiators or central heating.

I don't recall either of us crying. We had no choice, and we accepted our lot. We didn't know Cynthia or how to react to her. We did as we were told.

While we had been renting on Cannon Hill Road, Adrian, our brother, was born. I think with all of the responsibilities that Cynthia had, bringing up two small children along with a tiny baby and working, she was probably glad that her parents were close by.

Even though Cynthia moved us away, most of what I remember from my childhood in Birmingham is that time spent with Mummy and Daddy. She used to take us to school rather than Cynthia, and Mummy had a huge influence on my upbringing.

1969 – Lis

Going back into school to start in the lower sixth, my teachers did talk to me about trying to re-take maths. However, they didn't try too hard, they obviously decided I was a lost cause. Instead I chose typing and woodwork, the former being a skill I have made use of later in life.

I was lucky that I wanted to study at music college rather than university, because without a maths qualification I wouldn't have been accepted. A music college degree would get me into teacher training college for a one-year course. These days you need a maths qualification to start any teacher training course.

My A-level year began with studying English, Art, and Music. By the time the exams came along, I'd dropped English. Something I regret now, but at the time I couldn't cope with the sarcasm of the teacher. During one lesson he was talking about caesarean babies and said, "They have weak characters because they don't have to fight their way into the world. Of course, we haven't got any in here, have we?"

Being too honest for my own good, I put up my hand in affirmation that I was one such baby. He made me feel stupid and small, and this happened on many occasions. Instead of standing up to him, I gave in and left the class. I had been brought up to respect my elders, even if I disliked them and their behaviour. As I've matured I still battle within myself, but no longer respect people *just* because they are older.

Art lessons, on the other hand, were amazing and always on task, even though Mrs Wagner, our teacher, was liberal about allowing us to listen to pop music while we worked. She was a brilliant teacher who inspired all of us to find our styles and express ourselves. The majority of the art group went on to study at Art College; there was some real talent.

Years later, when working as a schools' adviser, I thought back to Mrs Wagner's lessons to inform my feedback when supporting an art teacher who was having problems. I wrote to Mrs Wagner to thank her and tell her how I was getting on in life. Sadly, I had a heart-rending letter in return from her husband telling me she had recently died, but how my letter had given him some comfort.

One massive advantage of being in the Leicestershire Schools Symphony Orchestra was the holiday courses. At Easter we always used to go away somewhere in England and in the summer we used to tour abroad. I was lucky enough to go to Germany twice with the orchestra before I went off to college, and the most memorable for me was visiting Berlin in 1969.

The Berlin Wall, which was initially barbed wire, had been erected swiftly in 1961. By 1969 the wall was built, a concrete division between West and East Berlin. Germany at the time was divided into two separate countries, East and West, with East

Germany run by the Soviet Union. Berlin was geographically in East Germany. As the capital of East Germany, the British, French, American, and Soviet Union ran it politically.

We travelled from the UK on coaches, with the instruments in the back half of the buses. When we got to Germany, we had to travel through a 'corridor' of East Germany to get to the Western sector of Berlin. It was a strange experience. We travelled along a badly-made concrete motorway, knowing that the land either side of us was East Germany; soviet-owned and communist, which in the 1960s was the nemesis of the West. The only traffic coming in the opposite direction was East German tanks, which added to our feeling of peril. This was the time of the 'Iron Curtain', and we had all watched those spy films about people trying to escape from the Soviet Union. Our young imaginations worked overtime.

At around midnight we arrived at a checkpoint, which was surrounded by a high, barbed wire fence. All of us were made to get off the bus via the driver's door, which meant that we had to be helped down by the soldiers as we clambered out. Our accompanying members of staff were worried that they might ask them to remove all of the musical instruments, which would have taken hours, and if not done with care could have caused a lot of damage. I remember feeling nervous, watching all these armed soldiers who were giving us teenage girls the eye. I accidentally snapped the toilet chain in the ladies and everyone was joking that they might shoot me. As stupid as it sounds now, I was genuinely scared, but of course the guards didn't even know about it.

After a few hours of searching our coaches and lots of paperwork being filled in, they allowed us entry into West Berlin.

Our German hosts took us on a trip into East Berlin, which meant passing through Check Point Charlie. For British teenagers it was an adventure without a true understanding of what it meant to the many Berliners who couldn't pop into the East to see family and safely return. I recall looking out of the coach windows and what struck me most was the lack of colour. All the buildings were grey. There were no adverts, no coloured paint, and few flowers. We were taken to a hotel for food and then to a park, where we visited a Soviet War Memorial Then we were back in West Berlin with its colour, beautiful green parks and sophisticated buildings and shops. We met German teenagers who had never seen a cow because, although they had a good standard of living, West Berlin was an island and they were unable to visit the countryside of West Germany.

That same year, we appeared on the BBC programme, *Omnibus*, in an episode entitled *The Other LSO*. It was both scary and exciting. Scary because we were being recorded live, and that meant that every sound including mistakes were picked up. Exciting because during the programme we were being put through our paces in a rehearsal by none other than André Previn. He had recently taken over as conductor of the prestigious London Symphony Orchestra. Being part of the LSO gave us all so many wonderful opportunities but, looking back, I don't know if many of us recognised how lucky we were. Due to the phenomenon that the LSO was, we were quite blasé about having well-known musicians working with us.

1969 – Conrad

The house on Canon Hill Road was always busy, with loads of people coming and going, music playing, and lots of fun. We spent as much time with Mummy and Daddy as we did with Cynthia, and these are the times I loved.

All the food we ate was Caribbean. We didn't eat much English food apart from on Fridays when there was a treat of fish and chips. Everything was cooked fresh with no additives.

Saturday was soup; this could be oxtail, pigs' tail, or soup with chickens' feet, (which I disliked intensely). Sunday lunch was traditional rice and peas, which for those of you who have not eaten it, is not purely a meal of rice and peas. Usually it is rice cooked to the particular recipe of that family, which could involve gunga peas or kidney beans as the 'peas' added to the rice. The recipe can also have chilli and coconut cream added. This accompanies chicken, again cooked to each family's own style. For the rest of the week we ate mostly a variety of Caribbean meals, but on Fridays, Saturdays, and Sundays the menu was set in stone.

Mummy and Daddy's house was a large,

Victorian terrace. There was a hall and on the left the best room which was used for visitors when I was older. When I was little the room was used as a bedroom for the lodger. There was a long, dark corridor leading to the living room and the kitchen beyond. There was a pantry leading off the corridor and Mummy kept the key close to her; she didn't trust anybody. Next to the kitchen there was a downstairs toilet, which I hated using because it was too scary and the corridor seemed to go on forever when I was young. Upstairs there were three bedrooms and the bathroom. We only had a bath at the weekends because that was when the heater was turned on for hot water. Because there were so many of us in the family, when one came out of the bath, the next would go straight in.

There were a lot of people in the house back then. My uncles, Danny and Cecil, shared a room, uncles Vincent and Gilly shared, and then there was the lodger downstairs. Dawn, cousin Sonia, and I shared the third bedroom, with Mummy and Daddy. The three of us slept in a large double bed, and our half of the room was separated by a large net curtain. Mummy and Daddy's bed was on the other side of the netting. Even with two double beds, the room was large.

There was also a large wardrobe and by the window Mummy's Singer treadle sewing machine. I was fascinated while watching her making clothes. She was incredibly quick as she moved her feet on the treadle and ran the material through her fingers and into the machine. An old paraffin heater sat by their bed, adding warmth to the room. Everything was flowery; the carpet, wallpaper, everything.

Where we lived in Edgbaston was a culturally and racially mixed society, so I grew up and played with other children from many different backgrounds. We also lived near two parks: Calthorpe Park and Cannon Hill Park that were great places to play and explore.

On Sundays everyone had to go to church, wearing his or her Sunday best, which meant suits and ties for the men and fancy hats for the ladies. This was the one time on the weekend when you dressed up. The church was Baptist, and as they didn't have their own permanent building, services were held in a school or hall. It was fun because there was a band with a guitarist, drummer, and pianist, and they played lively music that encouraged everyone to sing.

When you're young the services can seem strange because you see the adults stand up, sit down, stand up, sit down, or hold their arms in the air praising the Lord. People would stand up on their own when they got excited or in response to what the pastor was saying. Sometimes when all this was going on, we youngsters were so bored; we just wanted to go home.

When the sermon was taking place, the children used to be taken into a room of their own to listen to stories and learn about the Bible and the Lord's Prayer. I got a lot of my Christian values from my parents.

Unsurprisingly Mummy and Daddy's favourite music was Gospel, but I also loved listening to lots of different styles from an early age. I used to listen to the Birmingham Radio Midland Broadcast and its presenter, Jimmy Young. Every time any of my aunties or uncles came in, they'd see me with my ear stuck to the radio, so they started calling me Jimmy, and the nickname has stayed with me. The Beatles were big favourites too.

1970s –
World News

- 1970 world population: 3.707 billion
- The Beatles break up, 1970
- IBM introduces the floppy disc, 1970
- Bar codes introduced in the UK, 1970
- Idi Amin seizes power in Uganda, 1971
- US Supreme Court rules unanimously that busing students to be ordered to achieve racial de-segregation, 1971
- Intel introduces the microprocessor, 1971
- Britain takes over direct rule of Northern Ireland in a bid for peace, 1972
- Eleven Israeli athletes killed at the Munich Olympics, 1972
- The compact disc is developed by RCA, 1972
- Video Disk introduced by Philips, 1972
- Electronic mail introduced, 1972
- Great Britain, Ireland and Denmark enter the European Economic Community, 1973
- Richard Nixon resigned as US president – the first to do so, 1974
- Baryshnikov defects and joins the American Ballet Theatre, 1974
- Saigon surrenders and the remaining Americans evacuate, ending the Vietnam War, 1975
- Home videocassette recorders (VCRs) developed in Japan by Sony (Betamax) and

Matsushita (VHS), 1975

- First commercial Concorde flight, 1976
- Israeli commandos attack Uganda's Entebbe Airport and free 103 hostages held by pro-Palestinian hijackers, 1976
- Jimmy Carter elected as US president, 1976
- South African activist Steve Biko dies in police custody, 1977
- Queen Elizabeth's Silver Jubilee, 1977
- Ian D. Smith and three black leaders agree on transfer to black majority rule in Rhodesia, 1978
- First test tube baby, Louise Brown, born in London, 1978
- The Shah leaves Iran. Muslim leader Ayatollah Ruhollah Khomeini takes over, 1979
- Margaret Thatcher becomes UK prime minister, 1979
- Three Mile Island nuclear plant accident in the US, 1979
- Lord Mountbatten assassinated, 1979
- The Sugar Hill Gang release first commercial rap hit – *Rappers Delight*, 1979

UK Prime Ministers

Edward Heath, 1970-74
Harold Wilson, 1974-76
James Callaghan, 1976-79
Margaret Thatcher, 1979-90

1970s – Lis

My A-level music teacher asked me why on earth I cried when I got my A-level results. I knew why; I was so relieved that I'd got the grades I needed to go to the Royal Manchester College of Music. Not only was I fulfilling my dreams, but Mum's too.

I was in my element. Music every day and having complete freedom for the first time in my life! Our timetable was divided between instrumental lessons on our chosen studies, (in my case, my main instrument or first study, harp, and second and third studies, piano and singing), keyboard harmony, theory of music, aural, practical teaching lectures, and the history of music. The rest of the time was given to practising our instruments. It was heaven.

When I started the college was a mish-mash of old buildings, but in my last year we moved into the new building, which is now the Royal Northern College of Music. The old building was amazing, although something you might see in a bizarre dream. The main structure looked like a Victorian school. The entrance opened up into a large hall with a stage at one end and notice boards and stacks of chairs at the other. In between was the empty space where an audience would sit. There were various doors that led off the hall and disappeared into other corridors and teaching rooms. I didn't ever go through some of them, so they could have led anywhere. It reminded me of Alice in Wonderland with the white rabbit disappearing down dark burrows.

The students tended to be divided into two groups – singers at the stage end and everyone else at the notice board end. As a pianist, if you hung around in the main hall you could pair up with singers who often wanted accompanists. Even though initially I wasn't a first study pianist, because I could sight read easily I got asked to accompany singers, or instrumentalists, which I loved.

This building was on the corner of Dulcie Street, lined with small, two-up-two-down Victorian terraces, reminiscent of the opening credits of Coronation Street. These houses, which were also part of the college, were full of teaching rooms and when you ventured inside any of them there was a cacophony of musical instruments, mixed with singing voices. Often when I had my harp lesson in one of these rooms, my teacher, Jean Bell (the Halle Orchestra's Principal Harpist), would bemoan the 'bloody warbling' of the opera singers in the next room. Miss Bell was a dramatic lady in both speech and style. She had dyed, red hair, was always dressed completely in black, including a full-length cloak, and had large, round, red glasses that reminded me of an owl. This look was finished off with bright red lipstick. You could easily imagine her now as one of the teachers in *Harry Potter*. She spoke with a posh, loud voice, and always asked how 'Mamma and Papa' were. I was in awe of her and before her lessons I was either scared or nervous, but never complacent.

In my first year I shared a room in a house with another girl from the Leicestershire Schools Youth Orchestra. She was also called Liz, so because our names sounded the same we ended up with the nicknames, 'S' and 'Z'. Our room was in one of two large, terraced houses, each having three floors and a basement. The owner ran a martial arts clothing business. He only rented the rooms to girls and we weren't allowed male visitors. His presence was unsettling and we all found him creepy. It was worse for us, because he had a room on our floor. This was next to the bathroom that we shared with him and the two girls in the room opposite ours. None of us would have a bath if he was home because we were convinced he had a spyhole in the wall.

Although we weren't allowed male visitors, there was usually a hive of activity around 5.25pm every day prior to the owner coming home from work. You could move between the two houses by going through the top floor flat, if the girls were in, or through the basement. So, guys would be scurrying around to get to the other half of the house and out before he returned.

None of us wanted to lose our rooms because the rent was amazing value. We had a room with two single beds, a table and chairs, and a cabinet, which held both a record player and radio. We had shared use of the kitchen and bathroom and, in the basement, there were washing and drying facilities that were free. We didn't have to pay extra for our utilities, it was all in the rental, which nowadays sounds ridiculously cheap at £3 a week. Nowadays this equates to a whopping £43.11. The owner had twelve rooms, each housing two people, so he was making a good amount of money overall, and possibly the colleges paid him something too.

During the first week I shut the kitchen door rather too heavily and broke the mechanism that allowed the door to close quietly. Being scared of the owner, we wanted to get it mended before he came home, so we went and knocked on the door of the large house next door. We'd noticed a few guys going in there.

Norman, who was to become one of my longest and dearest friends, opened the door. He was studying to become an engineer. Perfect, exactly what we needed, someone who could mend the door. He, and his mate Steve, came round and while they repaired the door we found out that their house was part of a male hall of residence, Dalton Hall. Not having access to windows at the back of our house, we hadn't realised that Dalton Hall completely surrounded our house. Result! Norman became a great friend, and we spent much of the next three years together and have stayed in touch ever since.

Even when he had a girlfriend – which was most of the time – we all tended to go out as a group. Alongside the main building of Dalton Hall, the residence was made up of several houses around the compound. The house Norman and Steve lived in had a basement that was perfect for parties, which happened on a fairly regular basis.

Along with several other people, I used to draw large posters onto the pasting side of wallpaper that the boys managed to find. These posters were used to decorate the walls of the dark and drab basement. I used to copy album covers and iconic adverts of the time. People would take them home after the parties to decorate their rooms. I had a large 'Jungle Book' poster, painted by someone else, which I stuck onto the wall next to my bed. When it became unstuck and fell on me in the middle of the night, it terrified the life out of me!

In March 1971, Liz and I moved into a bedsit in Whalley Range, one of the less-salubrious areas of Manchester at that time. We had to share the toilet with other people in the house, which was gruesome, and we regularly had mice in our room. Although it meant we had moved away from Dalton Hall and all of the male students, our aim had been to move away from the house on Anson Road. No more rules and we could have any visitors we wanted.

It was that quiet, expectant time of the morning when it's neither dark nor light, but you know it's going to brighten up soon. The doorbell rang – early for visitors. I could hear hushed voices and then my Uncle Phil walked into the room. I don't remember exactly what he said now, and I don't think I heard then either. He told me that Dad had died. He was fifty-six years old.

It was a week before my nineteenth birthday and I think it was a Tuesday (we're not a family who hold onto dates of death or have memorials).

I didn't cry; I was too shocked. With Liz's help, I got dressed and packed some clothes. Uncle Phil drove me home to his house, where Aunty Dorothy was waiting to comfort me. From there I was put onto a train with my mum's Aunty Molly.

Aunty Molly didn't have children and she was

of the generation where you were expected to look after parents. As far as she was concerned I would now have to go home and look after Mum. As selfish as this sounds, I was as upset about having to leave college as I was about Dad's death. Music college was all I had ever dreamed of and the thought of losing it was as unimaginable as Dad dying.

When I arrived home. I was surprised to see how upset Mum was. She never seemed that 'in love' with Dad. She regularly belittled him and on many occasions she referred to me as *her* daughter rather than *their*, which I thought was sad. I didn't cry; I needed to be strong for Mum.

Dad had died in his sleep, which was good for him because he had never had a day's illness in his life, and he would have never had the patience to be a patient. I felt guilty for some time because the night he died I'd been out at a concert, enjoying myself and he was having his last day on earth.

On the day of his funeral I wore a blue jumper and a grey maxi skirt, because neither of my parents liked me in black. Also, I wanted to wear my favourite colour for Dad. The small church was packed with people. They were standing at the back and even outside the door leading to the small churchyard.

The service passed in a haze, followed by the trip to the crematorium. When the curtains automatically closed to hide the coffin, the mechanism squeaked, and it made me want to laugh. One of those serious moments where your emotions act opposite to way they should. We must have had people back for tea and sandwiches because that's what Mum would have done, but I don't remember any of it.

A week later I went back to college; Aunty Molly wasn't happy. I was neglecting my duties as a daughter. When I saw people I knew, knowing they were often lost for words, I would mention the funeral first and get it out of the way. Soon everyone had forgotten, and things carried on as normal.

Dad was mostly an easy-going man with a loud, infectious laugh. He sang with a rich, bass voice and always took the lead in the church choir when a bass solo was required. He didn't read music, so when he had to learn a new part I used to help him.

We were similar and as I got older we often clashed. He had Victorian ideas about children and, as far as he was concerned, I should respect him for the fact alone that he was my dad and elder.

On one occasion when I was home from college, we were watching an orchestra on TV and one of the flautists had an ebony flute. I commented on it and was told not to be stupid.

"You can't have an ebony flute," he said. "They're made of metal". I knew I was right, I had seen them at college. When I said this, I was told not to argue with your father. This stayed with me and I still get frustrated when I'm having a discussion and *know* that I'm right. It takes me straight back to that moment and the feeling of contained anger.

I annoyed Dad when I first got the right to vote and threatened to vote communist rather than Conservative like him. In reality, I didn't vote either way.

We shared a love of art and used to play drawing games together. I obviously gained my love of art and drawing abilities from him, definitely not from Mum who always drew stick men.

He didn't share the same sense of humour as Mum and me. He liked Tommy Cooper, and the silent movie slapstick humour of Charlie Chaplin, Buster Keaton, and the Marx Brothers, none of whom I ever found the slightest bit funny.

When I'd been little I had been a daddy's girl and would turn to him for comfort, but as I grew up I think he found it harder to understand me. Maybe he didn't like to see his little girl growing up. Mum often had to persuade him to let me go out with boyfriends. I think he'd rather have kept me locked up, as many dads would probably prefer to do with their daughters. He also wasn't pleased when I had my long blonde hair cut short and he persisted in calling me 'Bob'.

Dad and I did share a love of Westerns. Many Sunday afternoons were spent, much to Mum's annoyance, watching cowboy films on TV. I love watching them now, even the old ones with Audie Murphy, Joel McCrae, Randolph Scott, and Gregory Peck.

For a long time after his death I dreamed about seeing him. Walking down the street I thought I'd see him or recognise his walk in the distance. Looking back, I don't think I properly grieved for him. Writing and editing this section has moved me to tears each time as I realise how much I miss him.

A few months later, after returning to college

for my second year, I fell ill with glandular fever. They called it the 'students disease' because kissing passes it on. In my case the doctor said it was due to the emotional stress of Dad's death. I ended up having two months at home and missed out on a chunk of my second year. I was extremely lucky though as I made a good recovery and, apart from having a vulnerability to throat infections, I didn't suffer any long-term effects. Sadly, another girl in my year also had the same disease and lost her hearing; devastating for a musician.

Liz and I moved yet again into a ground floor, three-bed flat, with its own kitchen and bathroom in Edgerton Road, Fallowfield. This was a nicer area and full of students. Ruth, another student from college, occupied the third room in the flat. We had two pianos, my harp, and Liz with her oboe, much to the annoyance of one of our neighbours who was a nurse. If we did practice at home, we only ever did so during the day, but that wasn't much solace to her when she was working the night shift. Art students occupied the flats upstairs. They never complained about anything, probably because they were too stoned most of the time. The police even raided them on a few occasions.

I always had boyfriends, but as soon as there was any chance of sex I'd finish with them, or they with me. There were plenty of other girls who were more willing. Considering that this was supposed to be the new permissive era, when you could take the pill and sex was part of student life, I was still a virgin. When I'd left for college, Mum, seemingly the most uninterested person in sex ever, gave me 'the talk'.

"When you get invited back, or invite anyone back to your room make sure it is just coffee."

I was terrified of getting pregnant and letting Mum down, as she alone now supported me at college. But it wasn't only that. I was worried that when I had sex I'd do it wrong, or I'd look stupid, or it wouldn't work. I had been trying for years, unsuccessfully, to use tampons, so the thought of sex was scary to say the least. It was hardly surprising that I was nervous of having sex, when I knew my parents hadn't had marital relations for years, as Mum often reminded me. After I had been born they had been told that it would be dangerous for Mum to get pregnant again, and as birth control wasn't that reliable they chose not to have sex. I never heard Mum say anything positive about sex. In fact, she made it sound dirty.

Despite this, I had boyfriends on and off all the way through college. The funniest event was with a boy from the Isle of Man. He was six-foot-five, blonde, and very good-looking. I met him at a party and afterwards he came back for coffee. However, he hadn't had the 'only coffee' speech from his mum, and when I came back from making the coffee, he was sat on the bed in the briefest of red underpants. He was lucky I didn't throw the coffee over him with the shock at seeing such an Adonis on my bed. What was he thinking? In hindsight, it must have been embarrassing for him, when I made it clear he wasn't getting any sex that night, so he had to get dressed again. Although we did have a good night, I didn't see him again. I didn't really fancy him anyway. However, unlike most other guys, he didn't give up. He kept turning up or sending friends round to ask me out on trips. He was nothing, if not persistent.

The funny thing was that many of my friends who were having sex often asked my advice about their relationships. As if I had a clue.

During my three years studying at music college, I didn't go out with many musicians. Generally, they were too straight-laced, and the good-looking ones were often gay.

The classical musicians often didn't listen to non-classical music, which I found boring. Some of my musical friends wouldn't even come into my room when I played rock or pop. That was fine by me. I had, and continue to have, a broad taste in music. As well as classical music I liked Led Zeppelin, The Incredible String Band, James Taylor (who I adored), Neil Young, and many others.

I have always loved dancing too and whenever there was a party, disco or dance, I'd be there. I particularly liked dancing to soul music. Often when soul tracks were played, the dance floor cleared leaving only a few people dancing. I was always one of them. I found a lot of the beats of rock and pop too slow, whereas with soul music, I loved the funky rhythms.

At the end of our third year we were all rushing off around the country for interviews at teacher training colleges. I was accepted at Trent Park College, near Enfield, to train as a secondary school music teacher. All of my friends managed to find a place, but I was the only one to go down to London. Travelling to Trent Park College wasn't as straightforward as my journeys in Manchester had been, where I had either walked or cycled. Here I had to catch two buses and then the Underground. Once at college there was a long drive to walk down. There was an unspoken rule that if someone with transport saw women students walking alone they would give them a lift. On one occasion a friend and I got a lift in a Lamborghini driven by one of the professors. We loved it and enjoyed telling everyone about that for weeks.

I met my future husband at a party in my last term at college in Manchester. Graham was on the same engineering course as Norman, my best friend. I had gone to the party with Norman and his girlfriend at the time. Despite Norman being with his girlfriend, when Graham offered to take me home, he asked Norman if he minded, because he thought I lived with him.

It turned out that Graham's hometown was Derby, which isn't that far from Birstall, and we started going out together the summer we both finished college. He was tall, with dark-brown eyes and, like many students at the time, had long, wavy, dark-brown hair. We got on well and although we didn't have a lot in common we shared a love of films and the same sense of humour. Graham was much more into the outdoors than I ever was, and he loved cycling and motorcycling, the latter, I surprised myself by growing to love too.

Mum would only have been happy if I'd come

home with a vicar, a classical musician, or someone wealthy. So, when I turned up with Graham she wasn't impressed. In her eyes though, he did have one saving grace: a degree. Had he been alive I think Dad would have disapproved too. Mostly because of the motorbike, but I think the long hair would have come a close second.

His parents were far were more academic and philosophical in their outlook on life than mine. They had completely different values to my parents. One of the main differences between them was that they were staunch Labour supporters, whereas Mum and Dad voted Conservative. Graham's parents also loved the outdoors and cycling. Apart from the cricket matches Dad took part in, we rarely spent time outdoors, and visiting the great British countryside was almost unknown.

When I started teacher training college, we only saw each other at weekends because Graham was a graduate trainee for the Central Electricity Generating Board and spent his weeks visiting different power stations. He used to come and stay with me in Crouch End at weekends when Nicky, my flatmate, was away.

We hadn't been going out that long when he asked me, "What would you do if I asked you to marry me?"

I replied that I would say "Yes."

So, he asked me.

After telling his parents and Mum that we were engaged, we went off to buy a ring. I remember sitting in a lecture, fiddling with my new engagement ring and being conscious of it on my finger. Of course, it also meant that other people noticed it too, which is what I secretly wanted.

A few of us had got engaged around the same time and, with hindsight, I realise I was too young to be contemplating marriage. I often wonder if we all got caught up in the *idea* of being married and swept away by the whole dream and thought of future lives and children. Also, neither Graham nor I had slept with anyone before and perhaps we both felt that, having had sex with each other, that this was it. We were meant for each other.

One reality was that both Graham and I had older parents and had we lived together, 'in sin', as my mother referred to it, they would all have vehemently disapproved. I know that at the time we were in love with each other, but maybe if we'd not been so compliant with our parents' wishes possibly we would not have stayed together or even got married. By the time I finished my teacher training year, I was engaged with the wedding date set for the coming summer.

Amazingly, I passed my teaching certificate. I say amazingly, because I don't feel that I learned a lot during that year. We studied psychology, sociology, philosophy of education, and classroom planning but we needed longer in the classroom, and with much more structure than we had received. We weren't taught how to teach, just thrown in at the deep end and hopefully we swam.

1970-73 – Conrad

While Lis was beginning the three best years of her life so far, I was in my last year at infants' school. I attended Tindall Street Infants, a large Victorian building about fifteen minutes' walk from Cannon Hill Road. Generally, I was a good boy at school; mischievous and cheeky more than anything else. I didn't get told off at school much at all, probably because I was too shy to get into any real trouble.

My favourite lessons were sports. I loved running, tumbling and, in Physical Education, climbing the ropes, bars, running over the benches, jumping over the horse – anything where I was on the move and using my energy. Unlike Lis, I loved sports day and always took part.

Like most young boys though, I did get into some scrapes. Once I fell asleep on the desk with my head resting on my arms. I was awoken by people calling my name but didn't dare open my eyes. Because I thought I might be in trouble I pretended to be asleep and didn't move. At first, they thought I was dozy but then because I kept so still they were worried and called Mummy. Now I thought I was going to be in big trouble, but surprisingly she didn't tell me off. Instead, she took me home, recognising how tired I was.

On another occasion I found some red syrup in the kitchen that looked extremely tasty, so I drank it. It wasn't syrup; it was paraffin. I was taken to hospital where they siphoned the paraffin out of me. Everyone told me when I woke up I was crying, "Where's Mummy, where's Mummy?"

She always made feel so safe and the incredible love I had for her was given back to me completely. Daddy wasn't as demonstrative but when he felt like playing he would, and when he didn't, you were left in no doubt.

In 1970 the church my parents attended held its services in my school in Tindall Street. Being such a large building there was an older man who used to patrol the hallways and make sure everything was secure. He was tall and thin and wore round glasses, a suit and a trilby hat. As a small child, he was terrifying for some reason. The children used to call him the 'Duppy Man', which in Jamaican culture means 'ghost' or 'spirit'. When Mummy was with us we were brave, as long as we stood behind her!

The other person who used to scare us was Mummy's butcher, Sabu. We passed his shop on the way to school and he used to come out brandishing a meat cleaver to scare us. Even though he was on the other side of the road and it was unlikely he would ever catch us, we always ran past as fast as we could. He used to try to frighten all the children in the neighbourhood but whenever we went into the shop with Mummy he behaved himself.

In 1971 Cynthia moved us yet again from the place near the railway tracks into a new block of flats. The flat was on the third floor of a four-storey building called Balfour House, which was near the Five Ways roundabout. Dawn and I were pleased because it was a lot warmer and we didn't need the glass hot water bottle. However, it meant moving to a new school, St George Church of England Junior, Ladywood.

I was learning to tell the time and, even though I knew my numbers, for some reason I couldn't understand the concept of past and to. It all sounded like some fancy code that I wasn't part of. Cynthia was trying to teach me. I can remember the scenario as clearly as if it was yesterday. I was sat on the floor at Cynthia's feet.

"What time does that say?" she asked me, pointing to the clock face.

"Er..." I looked at the clock, struggling hard to recognise what it was. "Quarter past five?" I guessed.

That was obviously wrong, because a moment later I felt the clock bang into the back of my head.

"No", she said with frustration. "That's twenty to five, not quarter past five."

She pointed to a new time on the clock and before even answering I knew it would be wrong. I waited for the clock to hit me again, as it did every time I got the wrong answer.

I didn't cry even though it was painful, I just grimaced. I didn't know if this was normal behaviour for a parent. One thing I was certain of, I couldn't give the right answer. The same thing happened when I got spelling wrong too; only this time it was a book instead of the clock that hit my head.

I don't blame Cynthia in any way, I think she must have had other things going on in her own life that I didn't understand, or maybe this was how she had been taught. What I do know is, it did have a negative impact on my learning as I grew up.

Before Adrian was born it had been Dawn and me against the world. We were always together and were very close, even though, like most children, we did occasionally fight. We weren't jealous when Adrian was born; in fact, we were excited to have a little brother. However, he was always closer to Cynthia because she was around while he was growing up.

The three of us all had different fathers, so to make life less complicated, Cynthia gave us my dad's surname, McDermott. He was the only father of any of her children that she married. Even though Cynthia put clothes on our backs, fed us, and looked after us, Dawn and me weren't as close to her as children should be with their mother. To us, she wasn't our mother, Mummy was.

It seemed that each year Cynthia was moving us farther and farther away from the people we loved, our friends and the area that we knew. This time we moved to Quinton, which meant yet another flat and this time a council flat on the ground floor. It also meant another new junior school: Four Dwellings, Quinton. I couldn't understand why she kept moving us. With hindsight, maybe she was trying to better herself and make something of her life and ours. All we knew, as kids, was that we kept moving. I couldn't help but notice that in Quinton, there was a yet another change. More white than black people. However, we still went to church and, more importantly, we continued to see Mummy and Daddy. At least Cynthia didn't stop those visits.

Presumably, her parents had eventually come to terms with her behaviour when she took us from them.

A big difference for Dawn and me was in the way we lived with Cynthia. All the things that Mummy had done for us, Cynthia now started teaching us to do for ourselves. She taught us how to iron, wire a plug, set a table properly, and use boot polish to clean our shoes. Cynthia taught us these things so we could be more self-sufficient and take responsibility for ourselves. At the ages of eight and nine we each had a schedule of chores. We even had set tasks at weekends, vacuuming and tidying our bedrooms. Whenever we finished a meal Dawn and I would do the washing up always with a musical accompaniment. We would sing along together to make the time go quicker and make it more fun. We sang all the time and were always listening to music. Music was my escape.

It must have been an emotional time for Mummy and Daddy when, in 1973, Cynthia moved us to London. I was leaving Birmingham, the place of my birth for the unknown. I didn't want to leave Mummy but had to get on with it. You don't have a say in these things when you're nine. The view from our bedroom window in the new flat was of a graveyard; not the most exciting of views.

Sadly, I don't remember Cynthia doing normal, motherly things such as sitting cuddling me, or playing with me, or reading to me. I think that as a single mum she probably didn't have the time. When she left for work, leaving the three of us in the house alone, instead of being scared or worried, we were relieved because we could talk and play together. I loved it best when Dawn read to me, which she often did on these occasions. As Adrian and I lay in our bunk beds, she would read to us from the other side of the net curtain that divided our room. One of the books I loved most was about a bumblebee and his adventures outside the colony.

Sometimes, Cynthia used to send us to the shops to buy cigarettes, which wasn't a problem, but when she used to ask me to get a dozen eggs, that's when I would panic. I would be walking along thinking *what are a dozen eggs?* Often, I stood outside the shop petrified and scared, but I was too afraid to ask anyone what it meant. I didn't know if I should get one pack or two: 'get a dozen eggs' didn't compute. In the end I would guess. She had never taken the time to explain to me that a dozen meant twelve. She presumed I knew. Also, whenever Cynthia sent me to the shops on my own she never gave me a list and expected me to remember. She seemed to be totally unaware of my problems and that I got confused and couldn't remember what she wanted.

Living in London did offer some exciting moments. One day when Dawn and I were coming home from school we saw a big bright light in the distance. We were intrigued because it was summer time and we couldn't work out what this light might be, so we ran towards it. As we approached we saw TV lights, camera crews, and these three guys. We were both thinking, *who are they?* Then we realised:

it was *The Goodies*. They were filming an episode of their sitcom. When Dawn and I got back home, incredibly we could still see the filming from our bedroom. Eventually, we saw the episode on TV.

The new junior school I attended in London was Ealing Juniors. Throughout my infant and primary schooling, I was in the remedial class, which was a smaller group. We were taken out of Maths and English lessons to join the remedial group, but in other subjects we remained with the rest of the class. Luckily, I wasn't made fun of for being in the group. We knew why we were taken out of the larger class; because we were slowing down the rest of the kids.

Despite this, I used to love going to the library and reading books and that's how I helped myself to understand words and to read. I particularly loved fantasy, dragons, and fairy stories. I could understand words with no problem, as long as I could read at my own pace. The teacher in the remedial group was a lovely Scottish lady, who was tall with blonde hair. Sadly, I can't remember her name, but she understood exactly what we all needed. She cared about our learning.

On one occasion she took about five or six of the class, including me, to the Natural History Museum; my first time in Central London. The trip was fantastic and opened up my eyes to possibilities. I vividly remember walking into the museum and seeing the big dinosaur skeleton for the first time with its massive bones. I stood staring up at it in amazement. *Wow!* I thought, *It's unbelievable.*

Another time, she invited some of us round to

her house for tea and cakes and that made us all feel special. I'm thankful for this teacher who obviously cared for her pupils and wanted to give us new and exciting experiences that we weren't getting in our everyday lives.

Throughout my school life, I tried my hardest, but I found there were some things I could remember and for others my mind went blank. Every morning, first thing, there was a spelling test, which I hated. It didn't seem to be a problem for anyone else in the class.

Despite all of these feelings of failure, I always turned up at school. It wasn't through lack of trying, but I didn't seem to succeed. People didn't seem to notice I wasn't getting anywhere and so I was getting used to being classed as a slow learner or a dunce. Even Cynthia didn't seem to notice my problems.

One Christmas, because there were always too many children for the main roles in the nativity play, myself and another girl were chosen to be the tumblers because we were both so good at gymnastics. At the end of the performance all the parents were praising their children. All Cynthia said was, "Why weren't you one of the ones standing up there saying something?"

Nothing about how amazing my tumbling had been. Cynthia didn't even seem able to recognise my strengths and the areas I was talented in.

One area I excelled in was athletics; I could do anything and everything. I liked drama too, because you could pretend. I wasn't good at art, football, or cricket and I don't remember much about music lessons either. Outside school I loved listening to music and knew lots about it. It was something that made me feel happy inside. It was the one thing I responded to emotionally.

Although I was having problems in English and maths, I had no pressure from Cynthia. She didn't seem to be aware that I was struggling in some areas. Of course, as a child, I didn't hear the conversations she had with teachers, but she never asked me how she could help. I don't know if she cared or not. I assumed Cynthia saw me as a failure. She didn't say that in so many words. It was more what she didn't say, and I could feel her disappointment. Why haven't you…? Why can't you…? Or the words she left unsaid.

1974 – Lis

My teacher training year passed quickly, and it wasn't long before I was looking for a job. During the spring term I applied to the Birmingham Education teachers pool, where as a newly-qualified teacher they would consider you for any up-coming posts. Alongside job-hunting, Graham and I were planning for the wedding and looking for somewhere to live – a lot of new things all at once.

I loved Mum and we were close, but at times she stifled me. I felt she wanted to control my life and this often led to me feeling guilty if I wanted to do things she didn't agree with. Leading up to the wedding she was jealous of the time I was spending with Graham. She was annoyed that I didn't want to go shopping for her mother-of-the-bride outfit. I was probably being selfish too, because I wanted to spend my weekends with Graham, as I didn't see him during the week. Unlike brides of today who visit a variety of wedding shops to try on many dresses, a friend of Mum's made mine. We bought a dress pattern and the material for £9. The most expensive part of my outfit was my hat – a large-brimmed affair. Having fine hair, there was no chance of keeping a veil attached, so a hat was the fashionable alternative.

Mum paid for the wedding as neither of us had earned enough money at that time and we didn't want to wait until we had saved enough because Graham's mum had terminal cancer. We wanted her to be at the wedding, although sadly she died before the day arrived.

I'm not sure what Mum had envisaged for her only daughter's wedding. To help keep costs to a minimum the wedding reception was in a local pub. We were married at Wanlip Church where Dad's funeral had been two years before, and where, as a family, we had all sung in the choir. Most of the guests were family friends, who Mum wanted to invite as a thank you for their support after Dad's death.

I remember very little from the day, apart from being happy I was getting married to Graham. The day rushed by in a haze. Something that has always stuck in my mind is that I don't recall anyone telling me I looked beautiful. This doesn't worry me because I'm not a narcissist, but aren't all brides presumed to look beautiful? Isn't this the one day in your life you are supposed to look and feel like a princess? No one remembered to tell me. When photographing weddings I always make a point to tell the bride how beautiful she looks, just in case other people are too busy.

Our honeymoon night was spent in a pub near Leek, and then we drove up to Scotland in our Reliant Robin to a campsite in the grounds of Culzean Castle, Ayrshire.

When we returned, I started my first teaching job at Moor End Secondary School, Erdington, Birmingham. It was a small school by comparison to secondary schools these days. The Headteacher, Mr Thomson, ruled with a rod of iron. It was a co-ed school in a multi-cultural community. The pupils were fairly evenly split between white working class, Caribbean, and Asian.

Discipline was overly strict and at break times the pupils had to play in gender-segregated playgrounds. Due to the lack of opportunity to release their energy during break time, when the pupils returned to the classroom they were unable to contain any mischief that would otherwise have been expelled.

The classrooms were situated around a central hall and each room had a wall of windows that sided onto it. Mr Thomson would roam the corridors during lesson times peering into the classrooms through these large windows. Quite often he'd suddenly drop in, so you never knew when he was going to appear, which put all of the teachers on edge.

I had little to no musical resources and spent most of my time teaching singing lessons, playing recorded music, or giving the pupils musical quizzes. The small number of instruments I did have were old and totally inadequate for the job in hand and there was no budget for more.

This was the time when pupils could leave school at the Easter of their fifth year, and class 5.3 were the Easter leavers. Probably due to timetabling issues, or some other bizarre reasoning on Mr Thomson's part, class 5.3 were split into boys and girls for their lessons. This meant I had a class of three girls, and a class of seven boys, none of whom wanted to be in school a day longer. They certainly weren't interested in learning about music.

Mr Thomson required us to write out and hand in to him our teaching plans for the week. I wasn't coping with 5.3 at all so asked if the peripatetic Head of Music for the area could come and demonstrate a good lesson for me. The expert teacher turned up and couldn't manage the group any better than me, so after discussion with him we made the decision that I would write out a plan for Mr Thomson, but work completely differently with the class.

My biggest problem with the boys was keeping them in the classroom, especially when it was sunny. Basil, a gentle-giant lad of Caribbean descent wanted to be out playing cricket, and I almost had to stand in front of the door to try to stop him from leaving. In reality, the majority of the boys were taller and stronger than me. In the end I came to an understanding with the group that if they stayed in the room I'd let them work on the homework they had been given from other subject teachers and play them a record of my choice and one of theirs while they worked. If Mr T came into the room, they hid their homework. This is where the wall of windows worked as a positive; one of the boys would give us the heads up if they saw him appear. It worked. They stayed in the room and they got their homework finished, and I didn't have any more trouble. But so much for teaching music, which was why I was meant to be there.

The three girls were no problem at all, they wanted to chat to me about their probation officers, their lives, and being on the pill. Even though I was nearly ten years older, the girls had far more life experience.

During the spring term the School Inspector came to visit and observe all of us probationary teachers. The lesson where I was observed didn't go to plan. Due to another teacher being ill, I ended up with two Year Three classes, which meant that the lesson I had carefully planned went straight out the door.

At the end of the morning, one by one like naughty pupils, Mr T called each of us to his office where he told us we would fail our probationary year. The history teacher, who was also our mentor, had a room full of sobbing, upset young teachers at the end of the day. What else were we going to do with our lives; all we had wanted to do was teach? This was meant to be our career.

After my visit to Mr T's office, I spent the whole afternoon fighting hard to hold back my tears while teaching. I failed at that too.

Working at Moor End Secondary was the first time I came into real contact with people from Caribbean and Asian communities. As my first Christmas approached, I was expected to produce the big performance. Luckily for me, several of the older girls, including two pupils, Hyacinth and Claudette, loved singing and joined my choir along with several of their friends. I had the first successful Christmas concert of my teaching career.

At the end of the year I tasted my first Caribbean and Asian food, when several of the fifth-year leavers cooked the staff a meal, including curry goat, which was excellent.

1974 – Conrad

When Cynthia moved us to London, she didn't take us to the predominantly black areas such as Battersea, Brixton, or Southall. She wanted to live in a white area; in the suburbs. We couldn't understand why we weren't living within our own community as we had in Birmingham. Where we lived there was a mixture of cultures. However, 90% were white. I felt confused especially after living amongst a huge range of cultures in Birmingham. We had to accept the new circumstances. I adapted and soon had a mix of friends.

Even though I was born in England, when your family are from another culture, you have to live in both worlds. At home, what we ate, our use of language, the things we talked about, the music we listened to, and all the other traditions we followed, were from the West Indian culture. When you're out and about, you learn to fit in.

If a child is ever in a situation where they are removed from their own cultural background and traditions, there can be many physical consequences alongside possible emotional ones. For example: West Indians have to moisturise their skin and take care of their hair because otherwise both become dry in the British climate; it's not humid enough. A lot of English people in the 60s and 70s were unaware of these things.

One good thing about the move to London was that we were nearer to our favourite Aunty. We used to love going to visit Aunty Annette in Battersea. She worked in a clothes factory and was always bringing things back for us. She had a big flat and we always felt relaxed and were never told off like at home; it was brilliant. We wished that she were our mum, rather than Cynthia. Cynthia and Annette never got on and, sadly to this day, still don't.

Dawn and I had grown close in our formative years together and, although only a year older, she always looked out for me. When I started secondary school, there was an African lad in her class who started bullying me. Dawn is short, only about five foot, and this boy was nearly six foot and yet she challenged him like a little lioness. From that day forward he never bothered me again. Apart from this, secondary school wasn't difficult and even though I continued to be labelled as a slow learner and taught within small groups, I wasn't bullied.

Unlike my primary school experiences though I don't remember any specific teachers. I was finding it more annoying because I couldn't unlock my potential and at times felt stupid and embarrassed. Instead of taking my frustrations out in other ways, however, I withdrew into myself and kept quiet.

I belonged to a group of five friends, which included Jerry, who was also in the remedial class with me. The rest of them often used to bunk off school, but I never did. I even got the attendance certificate for having a good record; I wasn't a bad boy.

Jerry's house was right next to the school, but he was always late. It's funny how people who live nearest to school are always the ones who are late! After school our group would often go round to his house to watch videos or listen to music. Jerry liked the same music as me, including George Clinton who we had recently discovered and both loved.

At home, we were scared of Cynthia because she occasionally used to get dark moods. I now realise that she had huge pressures on her as a single parent with three kids and two jobs. During the day she worked as a midwife, and then in the evening she worked for an agency looking after disabled people. This meant we were latch-key children. She would leave us alone until she came back in the morning, telling us, "Don't open the door to anyone, and leave the light off."

We had to get ourselves ready for school and get our own breakfast. Cynthia, rightly, was worried about the authorities finding out there were children alone in the house all night. She was worried we would be taken into care.

Over the years, in between all of this work, Cynthia had lots of boyfriends. She was attractive but the relationships never seemed to last. She's been married four times but sadly has never really found happiness. Luckily, it didn't affect me at all having these different men around; it made no difference to my life.

1975-79 – Lis

After the first year of marriage and my first year of teaching, we left Birmingham for Gloucestershire. Graham had a job for the Central Electricity Board, whose headquarters were then in Barnwood, Gloucester, and I had a job teaching music at Tewkesbury Comprehensive.

Through the misfortune of Grahams' parents both dying the year we married, we had a deposit for our first house that gave us a good start on the property ladder. This was, amazingly, a detached, three-bed in Hardwicke, Gloucester, on the edge of a new estate. This house cost £13,000, which at that time was a lot of money but now with the soaring cost of houses sounds ridiculous.

Each morning during term time, I travelled to Tewkesbury on my Honda 90 moped, which was fine in the summer, but bitterly cold on frosty winter days. Our car was a bright pink, three-wheeled, Reliant Robin. Graham held a motorbike licence that also allowed him to drive a Reliant on the same licence. So, when I passed my car test, I also drove the Reliant. I know everyone finds them funny, but it was such fun to drive, as long as you didn't go around corners too fast! At traffic lights you could take off and leave everyone else standing but, of course, as soon as they gained speed, they left the Reliant standing! However, it got us from A to B both warm and dry.

After a couple of years, we decided to move to Tewkesbury and bought a four-bed town house at the end of the High Street. I loved the house. You could sit in the kitchen window, which was a tall square bay and watch everything that was going on in down town Tewkesbury!

The road we lived in was Twixtbears; so-called because the road was between two pubs – the Black Bear and the White Bear. Tewkesbury was a great place to live and particularly for Graham, as we were in walking distance of a number of excellent pubs. The town has always been known for its large number of pubs and, along with our friends, we used to frequent a few at weekends. Mostly though we used to go to the Berkeley Arms at the Cross. The Berkeley is minute and is full when there are forty people in there. The landlady at the time, Ruby, used to have regular lock-ins, but even after that closed, we'd move on to one of the other many pubs in

Tewkesbury, where there was a disco.

I mostly enjoyed teaching at the comprehensive, but got the most satisfaction from teaching the O- and A-level groups. These were the pupils that enjoyed and wanted to learn music. The third-years were another matter altogether.

The one thing that I've always had problems with is discipline. We weren't taught how to discipline pupils when I trained and being an only child doesn't give you the skills either. Unlike in bigger families, you're not involved in sibling rivalry or as many family disputes. Therefore, you've not seen how parents sort out conflict. When I had particularly bad kids or classes I wasn't brilliant at reprimanding them; I felt like swearing at them, which is neither professional nor helpful. Despite this, I did have some lovely classes, and particularly the exam groups.

Thirty years later I continue to keep in touch with two of my exam group pupils. We meet up at least once a year for a good chat and catch up. What is incredibly life affirming for me is that both of them have become music teachers. One remains in Tewkesbury and the other teaches in Hong Kong.

Sometimes at weekends I travelled to the Midlands to play with amateur orchestras in need of a harpist. There were several of us semi-professional musicians who would support orchestras with the more unusual instruments. Over time we got to know each other well and built up a real camaraderie.

Graham never joined me on any of these trips,

he preferred to go cycling or motorcycling. He also wasn't particularly interested in coming along to any of the musical activities that we had at the school. He did, however, accompany me whenever I performed in solo concerts, and always helped me to move the harp around, which was never easy. He also supported me when we sold my old harp to buy a new one, which was extremely costly, but stronger in both sound and build. However, because it was bigger it also meant buying a larger car. Harps are not the cheapest instruments to learn and perform with.

Because I wanted to develop my technique, I continued my harp lessons with Rob Johnson, the City of Birmingham Symphony Orchestra's (CBSO) harpist. I used to travel up to Birmingham for these lessons, minus harp, in my little yellow Mini. On a few occasions I played second harp to Rob with the CBSO when they performed at the Three Choirs Festival. This was nerve-wracking, especially when Rob played pranks on me by moving the pedals when I wasn't looking. This meant that when I played a chord it sounded completely wrong. He only did this in rehearsals, thank goodness, and I did eventually get wise to him.

Rob and his partner Peter came to stay with us once in Tewkesbury and poor Graham was mortified when they appeared for breakfast in their matching adult baby-grows (precursors to onesies), and stood in the full-length kitchen window to gain a view of the High Street.

1975-79 – Conrad

During the school holidays we always went back to Birmingham to stay with Mummy and Daddy, which we were always excited about. We couldn't wait; we used to pack our cases the night before and then because of our excitement we couldn't sleep. At least it gave Cynthia six weeks of freedom.

Initially Cynthia drove us to Birmingham but then she stopped, and we had to make the long journey by train and bus on our own. When we arrived at Digbeth bus station, Mummy and Daddy would always be there to meet us.

Prior to one journey we had told Adrian to go to the toilet before we left, because toilets weren't available on buses in the 70s. Of course, he didn't, so about half way he wanted to go to the toilet. We told him he'd have to wait and ignored him, and both started singing "La, la, la, la," so we couldn't hear him moaning. In the end he had to wee in a bottle!

During those summers, we weren't the only children staying in Birmingham for the holidays. Our cousins, Sonia, Tressa, and Evan were also there. We all paired up according to our ages: Evan and me; Dawn and Sonia; and Adrian and Tressa. We all slept together in the same bed, head to toe, in Mummy and Daddy's room. The six weeks always seemed forever; the best of times.

There was plenty to do too. We used to play out in the road and sometimes go to Cannon Hill Park where there was a centre to take part in activities like painting and craft work; all great fun.

Once, Evan, Adrian, and I entered a dance competition at Cannon Hill Park. Everybody who entered the competition had to dance to The Village People's *YMCA*. I won because I included lots of back flips, being good at gymnastics. I kept the trophy I won for years, in fact until I was nearly forty, so I was obviously proud of this moment.

On Saturdays Mummy used to take us all to the Bullring. In the 60s and 70s, the Bullring was an all-concrete monstrosity. Obviously the architects had a vision for what Birmingham city centre should look like and despite this oppressive building material, the atmosphere was buzzing and brilliant. Everybody and everything was there. I used to watch Mummy haggle with the men on the market stalls and they would always lose!

Edgbaston cricket ground parking was at the end of the road where my parents lived. Every summer when the cricket season started, people wanted places to park. To keep his parking space while he was at work, Daddy would get two chairs and put a ladder across them, and tell us to stand there and tell people, "You can't park there, that's our daddy's place." Because there were so many of us patrolling and watching the parking space, we easily managed to keep people away.

Each night, even though we were already in bed, we all watched the *News at 10* on ITV. Mummy and Daddy watched ITV because of Trevor McDonald, who was the first black presenter. I slept on the edge of the bed so that I could see around the dividing curtain and watch the TV. Obviously, I didn't realise at the time but this was when I was developing my love of current affairs.

The house was always full of different people, which meant there was always someone you could talk to and you were never alone. Having such a big family, we all played together and fought too, which is natural when you're growing up and finding your own way.

When Mummy reprimanded any of us, all she had to do was give us a look. That look meant everything; she didn't need words. She never hit any of us children but, when we were older, Daddy hit us on the arm with a leather strap.

Mummy used to make Daddy coffee with condensed milk, and a pinch of salt. Us four cousins would sit by his bed and wait for him to give us what was left. He would hand us his enamel cup, white with blue edges, and we would take turns to finish the leftovers. This coffee had a 'wow' taste.

Mummy used to wash the clothes in the bath; everything by hand for everyone in the house. She'd rinse the washing out by hand before putting it through a mangle. Then she hung them up; always piles and piles of clothes. Then of course she had to iron it all.

During the six-week holiday I used to help her wash, shop, and decorate. She was particularly good at hanging wallpaper. She didn't ask for help, but I was always there with her, like her little shadow.

Cynthia found a casting call in a magazine and,

after auditioning, amazingly, I got the part. I was twelve or thirteen and I performed the voice-over for a Rice Crispies advert. I had to say the words "Snap, crackle, pop!" with an African accent. Like all performances, I had to do it several times, seven in all. When the advert was finished it showed a black boy eating his breakfast with my voice speaking his words. It was my first acting opportunity and I loved it. The first time we saw the commercial on TV was when we were having breakfast ourselves. It was funny though, it didn't sound like my voice because, as well as the different accent, it sounded deeper.

Incredibly around this time, Cynthia paid for Adrian to go to drama school, which was an extra expense. I don't remember him showing any particular talent for drama, or it being a passion of his. I would have jumped at the chance because I loved dancing and enjoyed the advert experience. However, strangely, I wasn't jealous of Adrian, just excited for him. He never did anything with this training in later life, and now, as an adult, I know I would have if I'd been given that opportunity.

At the beginning of one of our holidays to Birmingham, Adrian and me had Afro hair-dos. There had been an explosion of the style due to Michael Jackson and the influence of American culture. A lot of the Caribbeans in the UK had the style. To make an Afro, you have to plait your hair, leave it overnight, and the next day comb it out until it goes frizzy, using an Afro comb to create the shape. When it rained, though, my hair always shrank back to its normal size.

When we arrived in Birmingham, feeling cool and proud of our hair, Mummy and Daddy weren't impressed at all. They wanted to know what is was, and marched us straight off to the barber shop. When Cynthia picked us up six weeks later, she was incredibly angry and had an argument with Mummy and Daddy for interfering. They had Christian values and didn't believe in long hair.

I had had four uncles who also lived with Mummy and Daddy. Danny, the eldest, had the nickname of 'Shortie', though his real name is Fitzroy. I looked up to him because he studied martial arts and used to train every day. Martial arts have always held a fascination for me. Shortie was at his peak, so I used to ask him lots of questions and he'd show me moves and how to fight with nunchakus. He even made me a pair out of wood.

The uncle after Danny is Cecil. He always used to dress well, and his Afro was always immaculate. He used to press his trousers and before he went out, he looked crisp; a phrase often used in 1970s Caribbean parlance. He was dapper and always serious, but super cool.

Vincent, the third uncle had a sound system made up of a large amp, which had big bulbs inside and was contained in a large metal box. Due to the weight of the equipment it took two people to carry it. You had the turntable to play the dub plates. The speakers were the size of wardrobes and it was these that gave the great bass line. The bass line was everything. You had to have a crew because there is so much gear to carry and set up. I used to creep out of the house to help him. Vincent's system was called Duke Wally, and everyone called him Wally. He used to play against Coxan, or Shaka in London. They'd have play-offs, (sound clashes) against each other. Back then what we now call rapping was called toasting. Someone would toast (rap) over the music on the dub plate. Vincent would travel to London to a recording studio where the engineer would mix tracks from a multi-track tape, onto a 10-inch acetate disc, which was the dub plate. He would return to Birmingham on the same day so the disc could be played that night. Dub plates are exclusive to each sound system. Each sound system had their own unique mix of creative sounds. If you had a dub plate, then people would know that you were good. He could hold his own against the other systems and was well known in the West Midlands. My parents used to tell him to turn the music off and they had loads of rows on the subject. It was through Vincent that I first got into Reggae music.

Gilly, the youngest uncle was a 'Jack the lad' and one for the ladies too. He was a cheeky chappie and forever getting into trouble. His mum always loved him though, and he was her favourite, despite everything. Whatever he put his hand to he was good at. In Calthorpe Park there was a sandy football pitch and Gilly used to create big drawings using a stick. He would draw huge pictures, such as Bob Marley and his dreadlocks, which looked amazing. He was good at music too. He could sing, rap, produce, and used to have a studio in Hockley. He knew the members of the band UB40 and once went on tour with them and Neneh Cherry. He actually got one of his singles on the radio when Pete Tong played it on his show.

Each of my uncles added different things to my life. There wasn't a favourite and they weren't even like father figures, but I looked up to them and enjoyed being around them.

In 1979, when the holidays were over, things returned to normal in London. Dawn was always unhappy and often tried to run away. She used to end up in Battersea, in the areas where there were more black people and where she felt more comfortable. Aunty Annette would always take care of her and then Cynthia had to go and get her back.

This year, though, she left for good. She secretly told Adrian and me what she was going to do. Even though we were close, and wanted her to stay, we knew it was what she needed. We helped her pack her suitcase and she went to Birmingham. She went to join Horace, a man she had met at a party. His Rasta name was Ruben and she found answers in his way of life that she couldn't find in London. She was trying to find out about black history and culture and had an emptiness that she couldn't fill. Like me, she also couldn't speak to Cynthia but knew there was something missing, and Ruben seemed to be her answer. So, Dawn left Adrian and me with Cynthia. Even though Dawn and I had developed a strong attachment when we were younger, I knew I would be all right without her. I was beginning to develop a strong sense of self even then.

1980s –
World News

- 1980 world population: 4.438 billion
- John Lennon shot dead in New York, 1980
- Iran-Iraq War began, 1980
- 'Pac-Man' released and becomes the best selling arcade game of all time, 1980
- MTV goes on air. The first video is *Video Killed the Radio Star* by The Buggles, 1981
- AIDS first identified and the first case diagnosed in the UK, 1981
- Riots in Toxteth, Brixton and Leeds, 1981
- Diana Spencer and Charles Prince of Wales marry, 1981
- Britain overcomes Argentina in the Falklands War, 1982
- Michael Jackson releases *Thriller*, the biggest selling album to date, 1982
- Channel 4 is launched in England, 1982
- Sony released the first consumer compact disc player, 1982
- Introduction of compact discs, 1983
- Motorola begins testing cellular phone service in Chicago, 1983
- Microsoft Word is first released, 1983
- Apple introduce the user-friendly Macintosh personal computer, 1983
- South Africa ends its ban on interracial marriages, 1985
- Race riots in Brixton after the shooting of

Dorothy Groce by police, 1985
- Availability of relatively inexpensive laser printers and computers begin to be commonly used, 1985
- The Nintendo Entertainment System is released in US shops, 1985
- Desmond Tutu becomes the first black Anglican church bishop in South Africa, 1986
- Voyager completes the first non-stop circumnavigation of the earth by air without refuelling, 1986
- After 28 years the Berlin Wall is torn down, 1989
- Chinese students take over Tiananmen Square and thousands are killed, 1989
- The Hillsborough disaster claims the lives of 96 Liverpool supporters, 1989

UK Prime Ministers

Margaret Thatcher

1980s - Lis

Most of my memories of the 1980s are of my job, houses (we had two moves in five years), and holidays. I can't, however, tell where we went, or when, as I always have difficulties remembering dates. Once something has happened I move on and I'm in the now. As a family we are not people who celebrate anniversaries of deaths, or other events as many other people do.

One event that did hit home personally was the Falklands War. One of my ex-students from Tewkesbury Comprehensive died. Matthew Stuart was killed on his eighteenth birthday while serving in the Royal Navy during the conflict. It was such a tragic loss: a lovely young man sacrificed for a lump of rock. I can't come to terms with the death of such young men and boys for political games that governments play out in the safety of their offices. I remember Matthew as lovely lad who was always polite and respectful, and had an obvious love of life. I feel so sad that he was robbed of the chance to develop into the wonderful man he was on the path to becoming.

My job at the time was as a peripatetic piano teacher, which meant travelling from school to school teaching piano. It was a fantastic job, which I loved, so when I was getting ready for Graham's Christmas party and had a phone call telling me I was going to be made redundant, I was devastated. I had got out of the bath to answer the phone, so got back in and, while having a good soak, started planning what I would do in the New Year. I was thinking that I could build up my piano and harp teaching and aim to get more performance work.

The phone rang again. Yet again, I got out of the bath to answer it. My boss was ringing back to say that he had some ideas and to go and see him in the New Year and not to worry; he had a plan!

In the New Year I began my new job as a classroom peripatetic. I continued to travel around schools, but this time only primary schools, to demonstrate to teachers how to teach music to their classes. I spent a year working at this job, which was frenetic. When a new music adviser, Brian Ley, was appointed he changed both mine and the other classroom peripatetic job titles to 'Advisory Teachers'. This was the start of ten years of the most exciting and inspiring time of my career. Brian had great plans for not only music, but the arts in general in Gloucestershire. Eventually we had a whole Arts team of advisers and advisory teachers in the visual arts, dance, music and drama. We were centrally funded at the time and the political climate in education meant we could support schools that needed help at no cost to them. It was definitely a golden time in education for me.

There were five music advisory teachers and we each had geographical and subject areas of responsibility. I worked with schools in the Forest of Dean and Cheltenham and with special schools countywide, as well as sharing responsibility for teaching the recorder throughout the county.

Each year when the new probationary teachers started we had the luxury of running a two-day creative workshop for the arts. Gloucestershire arts team was certainly on the map nationally. I was so lucky to have been a part of that team and to have developed the skills and experience that I did.

In 1984 we moved house yet again, this time to Highnam near Gloucester. The house was a new-build in Poppy Fields; the perfect address for me as poppies are my favourite flower.

We seemed to move whenever a house needed decorating. Graham wasn't keen on DIY at all; he was much happier being outside on his bicycle or motorbike. He didn't even like gardening, which fell to me, and I actually started to take an interest in the different plants.

As I reached the age of thirty-five we didn't have children, unlike the rest of our friends. I realised that if we were going to have children we needed to think about it now, but I loved my job and didn't want to stop working. Graham made the decision easier. He told me he didn't want kids, and if I did, maybe I should find someone else. Surprisingly he was serious about this, but no doubt he would have been shocked if I'd have taken up his offer to leave.

Growing up I'd always wanted a brother or sister and had assumed I'd have children. In my imagined life I had a large, vibrant kitchen full of my children with all their friends dropping by. I loved visiting friends from larger families whose households always appeared full of life. The arrival of children when you got married in the 70s and 80s was an expectation. However, now the thought of giving up my job wasn't appealing. If I had a child I would want to give up work. I didn't like the idea of missing out on the growth and development of my imagined child. Also, I knew that Graham wouldn't have wanted so much involvement and I didn't relish being a parent on my own. A general pattern for us was that when our friends had children we ended up losing contact with them, mainly because Graham wasn't comfortable around children. I was lucky, Graham had told me how he felt. So, I made my own decision. I wasn't desperate to be a mother. The decision was made: we wouldn't have children.

Surprisingly, we got no pressure from Mum. Because she was unsure of her late brother's disability, she always thought it might be hereditary.

We did, however, get comments from other people. One of my college friends, who had two children, told me I was selfish, and people often asked me in a judgemental tone why we hadn't got children. I would never consider asking someone why he or she *hadn't* got children. I wouldn't want to upset someone if their lack of children was due to medical reasons, however many people felt uninhibited in pressing us for an answer.

The other interesting thing I noticed was, when we went out with Graham's work colleagues I would often sit chatting with the men, for the simple reason that their conversation was more interesting than that of the women. I had nothing in common with their wives. I didn't want to engage in conversations about nappies or breast-feeding. I think some of the other women regarded me with suspicion because of this.

Neither Graham nor I regretted our decision and in answer to the charge of being selfish, I'd say we were less selfish because we made the decision not to bring children into the world purely because it's the 'done thing'. Neither of us were desperate to have them, so why do so? Why do people have children?

I'd argue that generally they either think it's expected of the them once they are married; they have an inescapable maternal or paternal urge to have them; they want to have children to inherit the family name; or they want children to look after them when they are old. I think if it is a maternal or paternal urge, then that is an important need to follow. I would question many of the other reasons; those appear as selfish to me as my reason for not having children appears to be selfish to others.

Our choice not to have children meant that we did have the income to take good holidays and spend money on our houses. After our move to Highnam, we moved to Cinderford in the Forest of Dean. It was on a small development of chalet-style houses. This was my favourite house of all I'd lived in so far. The lounge had a panoramic view of the forest that was stunning and the house itself had plenty of rooms, in fact too many for just two of us. It was beautifully designed and built; a place to be proud of. I loved the forest too. The people remind me of Northerners and don't suffer fools gladly. They say exactly what they think, but also make you feel welcome. The forest itself is one of the most magical places and its character changes with the seasons. It was the perfect place for Graham and his love of the outdoors. He loved going cycling and motorcycling, although that had its dangers, mainly in the guise of the kamikaze sheep that have a tendency to unexpectedly leap out onto the road.

Graham and his family had always taken camping holidays and, although we had done this a few times in our youth, we had over the last few years tried organised holidays through agents; something Graham would never have considered in the past. Our first such holiday was a small group tour to a place called St Nikola on the Danube River in Austria. The holiday was only for a week, which was good. Due to the type of tour, we spent most of the time with the same, small group of people. Some we got on with very well, and some we didn't take to at all, so steered clear, which wasn't always so easy in such a small group.

We did have some fantastic days out including a wonderful boat trip to Melk Abbey, which included a stop at Durnstien, said to be where Richard the Lionheart was imprisoned on his return from the Holy Wars. Another day we visited Linz, and we also travelled to Vienna for the day. After a wonderful day in Linz and on the way back we went to visit the Mathausen prison camp memorial, which had a profound effect on everyone. Our day in Linz had been lively and our journey on the coach had been fun. The trip home from Mathausen was anything but; we were all profoundly moved and saddened by what we had experienced. The Mathausen Memorial was a brief, though extremely chilling insight to the memory of the atrocities that took place there. As we walked around the buildings I was overcome by an immense feeling of grief, so much so, that even now I can't recall what we actually saw. The impact and atmosphere of the place gradually instilled a feeling of deep sorrow and inner questioning of just how one set of humans can carry out such acts of cruelty on another. All of us were quiet, and the lively group of people who had disembarked from the bus were struck dumb on their return journey. I don't remember any conversation taking place.

After this trip, we decided to try a different country and we had a wonderful holiday in what was then Yugoslavia. We stayed in Bled in Slovenia for a week and then travelled to Hvaar, an island in Croatia.

We both decided we loved Austria, so we spent several holidays there in the future. We liked two-centre holidays, where after a week in one place we'd move on to another and usually at least one of these was a lakeside resort. Graham loved walking, and I loved being on boats, so these holidays were the perfect combination.

1980 – Conrad

Christmas, 1980, I couldn't believe what my present was: a bike! Not a racer or anything fancy, just a Raleigh, but still; a bike.

One of the boys at school had joined a cycling club that went out for rides on Sundays, and I asked him if I could join too. This boy was a natural cyclist, who had a racing bike, and I don't think he wanted me in his club. Even though my bike wasn't a flashy racer, I took great care of it. It wasn't the fact that it was heavier and wouldn't go as fast; I would just pedal harder. When the club met for exercise this boy would tell me a different night for the practice, but I managed to find out and joined in. Whatever route they took, on the ride back there was a long stretch of road which passed RAF Northolt. As you came down the hill you just went for it. Even with my bike, I never gave up; I gave as good as I got.

One Sunday during a ride I was falling behind the rest of the riders. It had been a long ride, and my legs suddenly went weak and in the end I fell off my bike. The club rode off, leaving me in the middle of nowhere. Pushing my bike, I managed to walk to a local pub. I must have looked a weary figure as I walked into the all-white pub. They welcomed me in; sat me in front of the fire, put a blanket round me and gave me a hot chocolate to drink. Then they very kindly took my bike and me to the train station. These strangers treated me better than the group of cyclists I'd ridden with for the last few weeks!

When I got back to Northolt I had to walk under a subway. As I wearily pushed my bike in front of me, I saw three white guys walking towards me. Because of my tiredness, my imagination ran away from me. This wasn't the countryside, and they looked a bit menacing to me in my overly-tired state. *If they beat me up, they beat me up, I don't care,* I thought. They walked past totally ignoring me. To be honest, things didn't generally happen in Middlesex, it wasn't like other parts of London, where sadly I might have been beaten.

One day in the school playground I started violently retching, and then eventually I threw up, but only bile. For about a week I couldn't eat anything at all, and even the smell of food made me heave.

Cynthia kept me off school for the week, and

took me to the doctors. He thought it was just a stomach bug, and prescribed Gaviscon Syrup. Little did I know that this was the start of a problem that would continue until I was well into my late twenties. Each year I'd end up suffering with crippling stomach pains and sickness and having to take at least a week off work. I tried many different diets but nothing alleviated the problem.

At sixteen, after being enthused by my Uncle Shortie, I started studying martial arts. First Judo and then Karate, and then Wing Chung, which is close combat fighting. Bruce Lee was the last person to be trained by Yip Man who was the Master of Wing Chung (although it was a woman who created it and Yip Man mastered it). Bruce Lee was and is one of my heroes, along with Jackie Chan, and I would always make the effort to see their films. I was particularly excited when *Enter the Dragon* appeared on TV for the first time in the 1980s, as I'd been too young to see it in the cinema when it was released in 1974.

One of my friends around this time was Richard, who had freckles and ginger hair. He lived in another block of flats in the same area and we had been best friends since junior school. We used to play computer games together at his house, particularly the tennis one called *Pong*. When we went to secondary school, he went to Northolt High School and I went to Walford High School, but we kept in touch. Then Richard joined the army and we didn't see each other after that. Several years later I bumped into him in the street. He'd changed a lot and when in conversation I mentioned I was going out with a girl, whom Richard knew was white, he shocked me by saying he 'didn't think races should mix'. This was totally different to his thinking when we had been friends. He continued, "People should stick to their own kind." Sadly, a year later I heard from someone that Richard had died in the Falklands War. That was a shock because we were the same age; one minute he was there and then not, and I could clearly remember our childhood together. This was the first young person who I knew who had died before their time.

I was working at McDonald's but was still having problems with my learning. Although it was frustrating not knowing why I couldn't always understand, I did always try anything and everything, the same as everyone else. I seemed to be slower and was always the last one to answer a question. This meant that I was afraid to work on the tills because it made me feel pressured when I had to do things quickly while someone was waiting for change.

This was my first full-time job after leaving school. I wore a brown uniform with flared trousers and one of those silly paper hats that wouldn't stay on my head because of my Afro. McDonald's had excellent training modules with a structure where you could see how well you were progressing. You had to learn to use the machines and get five stars on each one before moving on to the next. From there you could become a floor manager where, in place of the uniform, you wore a shirt and tie and had more responsibilities. McDonald's even had a university and if you wanted to get further there was the possibility of running your own branch

There was a special way to flip the burgers when you worked in the kitchen and I became an expert 'flipper'. To start with, I watched the other guys to see what they did. They would have five burgers stacked in each hand and then they put one from each hand on the grill so they stuck and then quickly slap down the remaining ones in a line from the first two. You had to press the buzzer and when the second buzzer sounded you'd quickly flip them. I became expert at this and had a bit of flair too. It was great fun, and we had a brilliant crew. Working there boosted my confidence and I was made to feel I could do anything. There was no limit to what you could achieve. When other branches were in trouble, staff from our branch used to be sent in to show them how we worked as a team.

I also met my first serious girlfriend, Frankie, while working at McDonald's. At seventeen I had sex for the first time too. I didn't particularly enjoy it the first time, even though it wasn't Frankie's first time. People have high expectations about what sex is going to be like, but my first time wasn't that good. You have to know your body, how to breathe and build your technique. Practice, practice; lots of practice!

So, that's what we did at every opportunity when Cynthia was out. One time she came home early, and we were in my single bed. For some reason, Cynthia came into my room to talk to me. I told Frankie not to move and, as Cynthia started talking,

I sat up to block Frankie from her view. Frankie did exactly as I said. She hid under the quilt and kept totally still, not moving an inch. Had Cynthia found us, we would have been in trouble with a capital T. We had to wait for Cynthia to get changed and go out again before Frankie could leave.

Over time, I fell in love with Frankie. When I was with her family both her parents and sisters accepted me, but I knew I could never introduce her to Cynthia. I would have been met with only disapproval. She knew I was going out with Frankie and I did take her home once, but Cynthia was most surprised with the colour of her hair, which was bright red. Frankie was heavily into the New Romantics at the time. Cynthia didn't understand. I always felt comfortable around other families and forever wished that mine could be the same.

Despite Cynthia telling me when I was younger that she didn't care whom I went out with as long as they were clean and nice, in reality she meant as long as they were black.

When I went clubbing I danced to soul, rare groove, funk, and jazz and although I saw both black and white girls, I always ended up with white girls. After all, I had grown up in a white area with white friends and as a young teen growing up, when, like other boys I looked at porn magazines, all the women were white; it was rare to see black models. The only time I saw black women that I was attracted to sexually was in movies, and they were always strong women.

Unsurprisingly then, my girlfriends were white,

so I was always torn between who I liked going out with and who Cynthia expected me to see, which is why I never took girlfriends home.

During the 80s, I went to college to study electronics but, yet again, I couldn't keep up with the rest of the class. Anything to do with theory caused me problems. I could understand it but only at my pace, which wasn't the speed of everyone else. People automatically think 'you should know that', but why 'should' you? However, practical, hands-on stuff I found easy.

I went for a job in the Marks and Spencer warehouse, and, as part of the interview there were multiple-choice questions. I panicked and didn't finish them, so again I wasn't accepted. There are lots of kids out there who have learning problems but don't ask for help because they're embarrassed and then they end up lashing out in frustration. You either do that, or you learn to cope. I learned to cope. To this day I don't like quizzes, they make me panic and freeze, even though I could actually answer many of the questions, particularly those on sport, music, and world affairs.

Someone had told Cynthia that if she worked abroad she could earn good money, so she applied to do midwifery in Saudi Arabia. They had a shortage of nurses and had built several new hospitals, but then, of course, needed people to work in them. The money was tax free, and she got paid trips home a number of times a year. In 1982, Cynthia was offered the job in Saudi. About this time, she also gave me an ultimatum: if I kept seeing Frankie, (because she was a white girl), I couldn't live under her roof!

She was always giving me ultimatums, so, this time, I left home. I stayed with Frankie and her family for about a month. Her parents were lovely and a real family unit who always made me feel welcome.

Eventually I got my own bedsit in Southall and was working in Asda near Acton, and even had my own car; a Triumph Dolomite. I had money in my pocket and was taking care of myself. Cynthia thought I wouldn't be able to cope and would come rushing back, but I didn't. Gradually, I progressed in my work in Asda and was promoted to the position of supervisor of the produce department. I had people working under me and they respected me because of the work I was doing. I had learned to use my strengths, and it worked.

I have always loved dancing and that came before girls. I went clubbing to dance, not to pick up girls. When I worked at McDonald's my friend Brian and I regularly went to several clubs in the area, including the Electric Ballroom in Camden. Later, when I worked at Asda, I used to go into London.

It was the norm to have 'spotters' for TV programmes, in particular the UK version of Soul Train. These 'spotters' would watch the clubbers dancing and then hand out tickets to people they wanted to dance in their audience. Brian and I got tickets for Soul Train at least four times. On our first occasion we went to the studio and danced our socks off. Then the producer came up to us and said, "That was great, can you do it again? We're going for a take this time." Having given our all, we were both out of breath, but had to do it all over again with the same enthusiasm.

Frankie had stopped seeing me because she had met someone else, and it broke my heart. I felt betrayed and hurt and, after she broke the news to me, I sat in my car crying. That changed me a lot and it stopped me from opening up to people again. I didn't go out with anyone for four years. My whole attitude changed and, because I couldn't be with who I wanted to be with, Frankie, I started seeing any girl and didn't care much about any of them.

When Cynthia was preparing to leave for the job in Saudi, she realised that she hadn't got anyone living in the flat with her. At the same time the opportunity arose for her to buy the flat she was renting. Having thrown Adrian out, and Dawn having left several years earlier, she needed someone to live in the flat while she was away. Somehow, she managed to persuade me to return.

My relationship with Cynthia was strained to say the least. I was maturing but couldn't talk to her, even though she was always telling me to speak to her. At the age of eighteen, I had ended up in the flat alone with Cynthia. She bought the flat, put both of our names on the mortgage, and left for Saudi. On leaving she told me that, "On no circumstances are you to let Adrian come back." I was too scared of her so I only let him visit, never stay.

Each month Cynthia sent me money, which I put into the bank to pay the bills. It wasn't easy. I was trying to keep on top of the finance along with everything else on my own, without any guidance. A huge responsibility for me at the age of eighteen, and particularly when I found maths so difficult. Somehow, I generally managed to cope.

One time, the phone line was disconnected and I didn't know what to do. The reason it happened was because Cynthia had arranged for some chairs to be upholstered and the company wanted paying. She hadn't planned for, or sent money for the extra expenditure, but I didn't know that and paid for the chairs. She had set up everything to be paid by standing order and direct debit but hadn't thought to explain any of it to me. I bought my own food and things I needed with my own money but, increasingly, I was becoming more stressed with the added pressures from Cynthia.

I spent several Christmases on my own, which didn't add to my feelings of wellbeing. After all of this, things were beginning to get too much. I was in the flat on my own staring at the four walls. I also hadn't got a job at the time and was finding it hard to cope.

Browsing through a magazine I saw an article about a kibbutz in Israel and thought that might be something I could do. I even considered joining the army to get away and escape. I didn't know what to do and had nobody to talk to or turn to. I was too scared to talk to Cynthia because she would have called me a 'useless boy', and her negativity towards me would have reinforced how I felt at the time. Mummy was in Jamaica, so I couldn't easily talk to her either.

Then, amazingly, the phone rang; it was Dawn. She talked to me for an hour and suggested I went to join her in Birmingham. I was torn. I was worried about leaving the flat and bills, but Dawn asked me if I wanted to stay stuck there or get away. It was one of the hardest decisions I'd had to make in my life so far. I could stay, I could go to Birmingham with my sister, or go to High Wycombe where my then-girlfriend, Jackie, lived. I chose Birmingham.

Dawn travelled to Northolt on the coach to collect me. I had packed all of my clothes and belongings into ten plastic bags and one soft holdall. Feeling anxious and scared, with my stomach churning, I closed the front door and put the keys through the letterbox. There was no turning back.

I never did know what Cynthia thought about my hasty move. She didn't get in contact with me, and as far as I know, the first she knew about it was when she arrived home to the flat and found a pile of letters and my key. My brother, Adrian, was regularly in touch with her, and he just said, "Mum's really angry with what you did".

When we arrived at Victoria Bus Station Dawn persuaded the rather disgruntled driver to let us put the plastic bags into the luggage space and we were off on our journey to Birmingham. Back to where I had spent my happiest days.

My sister hadn't thought about what we'd do next. She hadn't considered where I'd live, or how I'd manage. Her aim was to get me away from Northolt, which she had done. I stayed with her for about six months. I signed on and when I got my first giro I even changed banks because I wanted to start afresh. Next, I managed to get accepted onto an access course to train as a mechanic. I finished the course and then the Job Centre knew people who wanted trainees, so I got a job.

I managed to get my own flat from a local housing association, which happened to be across the road from my sister. Once I had the flat, I furnished it; carpet, wardrobe, sofa bed, TV, cooker, and it was all mine. Since leaving London, I never looked back; I was free at last and could get on doing what I wanted to do.

One of the best things about moving to Birmingham was that I got to know my sister's children, Charmaine, Irene, and Jahdai. During the months that I stayed with them, I used to babysit for Dawn, which meant that the kids and me had time to get to know each other well. We had so much fun. When we played hide and seek, I used to hide in a cupboard and they thought I had vanished. I also taught them how to dance. They used to dance in the kitchen and would try hard to copy me. Whenever they visited my flat I always used to have lots of sweets for them. They also used to help me count the one and two pence pieces that I'd saved in a large whisky bottle.

Considering that I was in Sparkbrook in Birmingham and not in the countryside, when I ate my breakfast, I could look outside the kitchen window and watch squirrels playing. At last I had my own space; a small studio flat but all mine, and I loved it! I felt in control of my own life.

1990s –
World News

- 1990 world population: 5.279 billion
- South Africa free Nelson Mandela after 27 years in prison, 1990
- Communist Party relinquish sole power in Soviet Union, 1990
- South African parliament revoke apartheid laws, 1991
- Bill Clinton becomes President of the US, 1992
- European Union is founded, 1992
- CDs surpass cassette tape sales, 1992
- Two policemen convicted in L.A. on civil rights charges in the Rodney King beatings, 1993
- Stephen Lawrence stabbed to death in an alleged racist attack, 1993
- World wide web is born at CERN, 1993
- First human cells cloned, 1993
- Thousands die in Rwanda massacre, 1994
- Nelson Mandela elected President of South Africa, 1994
- IRA declares cease-fire in Northern Ireland, 1994
- Fiftieth anniversary of the dropping of the atomic bomb in Hiroshima and Nagasaki, 1995
- Ebay is founded, 1995
- First cloned sheep, Megan and Morag

created in the UK from embryo cells, 1995
- Dolly the sheep is cloned, 1996
- Hong Kong returns to Chinese rule, 1997
- J. K. Rowling's *Harry Potter and the Philosophers Stone* is published, 1997
- Diana, Princess of Wales is involved in a car crash in Paris and later dies, 1997
- Scotland votes for its own parliament after 290 years of union with England, 1997
- Wales votes in favour of devolution and the formation of a National Assembly, 1997
- Europeans agree on single currency, the Euro, 1998
- Google Inc. is founded, 1998
- Sky Digital is launched in the UK, 1998
- First Welsh Assembly in over 600 years opens in Cardiff, 1999
- First version of MSN Messenger is released by Microsoft, 1999

UK Prime Ministers

John Major, 1990-97
Tony Blair, 1997-2007

1990-92 - Lis

We were living in Down Ampney in a beautiful, detached house, surrounded by a dry-stone wall. I had been excited about living there because it was the village where one of my favourite composers, Ralph

117

Vaughan Williams, was born. None of the houses in the village had numbers, only names so, because ours was a new-build, we got to choose its name. We called it 'Larks Hey' referencing Vaughan Williams *Lark Ascending*. It was a sleepy village with a little shop and a church and a small primary school. (It has since had some new development and grown.).A Quaker family owned the land in and around the village, so there was no pub that Graham could walk to, much to his disgust.

We'd moved yet again due to Graham's company moving to offices in Swindon. We had searched for houses everywhere in a twenty-mile radius and eventually found this lovely house, built by a local builder for himself and his family. After it was finished his wife decided she didn't want to move from where they were living.

Life in Down Ampney was good, although for me a little claustrophobic. In a small village everyone knows everyone... and everybody's business. I was a member of the church choir and, after a short time, became the choir mistress, strongly supported by one of the tenors, who was also a serving officer in the RAF. Between us we organised the Christmas carol service and planned other musical concerts. I was often selected to play the church organ when the organist didn't turn up. This was something I hated, because I don't like playing the organ – it's a completely different technique to playing the piano.

As the Forest of Dean had previously been, this was a perfect spot for Graham. He could go off into the country on bike rides, and when the weather was good, it was perfect for getting out on the motorbike too. Well, near-perfect because of the lack of a local pub.

Another great advantage about living in Down Ampney was that when the Air Tattoo was on, we could sit in our back garden and watch the planes fly over. In our second year in the house, however, the sort of planes flying over were completely different. They were active B52s leaving to bomb Kuwait. You didn't want to imagine what would happen if they didn't quite make the runway when landing.

I started having trouble with my stomach again – well actually, my bowels. I used to suffer from excruciating stomach ache and could actually feel a lump in the lower part of my belly. I'd been told it was wind and had been given powders to alleviate the problem. When we moved to the Cirencester area and to a new doctor, he sent me to the local cottage hospital for tests. I was booked in for a barium enema x-ray. It was as horrible as it sounded. The worst thing was the stuff they give you to empty out your bowels the day before. You spend your time drinking the awful-tasting preparation and taking lots of visit to the loo.

Off I went to the x-ray. I wasn't worried; I'm always an optimist. My thinking was that if it was anything serious, I'd have lost weight. The x-ray wasn't so bad after all, but they kept asking me if I'd drunk all of the preparation, to which I replied 'yes'. Afterwards, they were lovely, and made me a cup of tea before sending me home. A little while after returning home, I received a call from the hospital asking me to go in the next day, they'd had a cancellation, and so the consultant could see me. I was impressed. Remember, I wasn't worried; I'm an optimist.

The consultant showed me my x-ray. He pointed out a large lump, the size of an apple, sitting in my colon.

"Usually a lump this big is cancerous," he said.

I sat listening, feeling sicker and sicker, though remember, I'm an optimist, so I heard the word 'usually' with hope. I left his room with a date for a hospital bed and a biopsy the following Monday morning. On the drive back to work every song on the radio seemed to have the words 'dying' in them, including one of my favourites, Prince's, *I would die 4 u.*

When I eventually got back to work, according to my friends, I was as white as a sheet. Graham didn't take the news well and, in his mind, it was terminal and he already had me six foot under.

After the biopsy, it was found that I had 'unusual cells' that if left had a high chance of turning to cancer, so an operation was planned to remove the offending lump and surrounding area of colon. This was my first hospital stay in my whole life, at least since being born.

The operation was a success, and I was extremely lucky as they only needed to take away a small part of my colon so I didn't need a colonoscopy bag, or any radiation therapy.

The most amusing thing, which still makes me laugh, was that after the operation (during which my digestive system had closed down), they had to wait for me to pass wind before I could eat solids. All the other ladies in the ward felt guilty when they were fed solid food and I was getting sustenance through a drip. So, when I farted early one morning, there was a cheer from the other beds around me! Some years afterwards I remember hearing that the reigning Pope had the same operation, and it amused me to think of them waiting for His Holiness to fart!

During my hospital stay an amusing misunderstanding occurred. Amongst my visitors were three vicars that were friends and acquaintances at the time. An old lady in one of the other beds made the connection that I might not be at all that good, as I heard her tell a friend in a stage whisper. She thought the vicars had come to see me because I wasn't long for this world.

Having fully recovered, I decided I'd give more time to my life rather than work but, to be honest, that plan didn't last long. I loved my job, and I was soon back in the swing of things.

Some say that life begins at forty; but it would be cruel of me to say that, because I had a good life with Graham and he is a lovely man with whom I had eighteen years of happy marriage.

At my annual music conference for education I met someone who I was attracted to and spent most of the weekend with. It was great being able to talk about music and art with the passion and get a similar response. We didn't have sex, but there was an obvious mutual attraction.

Graham and I slept in separate rooms and had

done for years. We had lived together for several of our eighteen years as best friends and hadn't been lovers for a long time. I think had we lived together when we were young we would have split up sooner, but both having older parents that was out of the question. We were in love, so we got married. That was the expectation.

After being attracted to this other man, who I'll call Dan, I came back from the conference and set about trying to seduce my husband. It didn't go well. I began to think about my recent health scare and that I didn't want to die without having sex again. I was forty, and had plenty of years left for a healthy sex life!

I spent weeks with so many thoughts and decisions going around my head. I talked to my closest friends wanting to find the right conclusion for both of us. I even tried to make Graham dislike me by being short with him, but it didn't work, because he is too nice. My idea was that if he started to dislike me it would make it easier when I told him how I felt. I thought I was being selfish on one hand but then, on the other, I would have been selfish to stay when I wasn't fully committed to him.

Eventually I did the hardest thing I think I have ever done. I told Graham I wasn't in love with him anymore, and that I thought we should separate. It was hard because we were great friends, and I knew I was hurting him. He was, unsurprisingly, devastated. He couldn't believe that I wanted to go but, as hard as it was, I knew in my heart and head that I needed to.

Sitting there in the kitchen, both of us in tears,

was surreal. This was the man I'd been with since I was twenty-two. The man who I'd grown up with. Who I'd supported and shared so much with – the loss of both his parents; who supported me through my career and now I wanted to set both of us free to grow new lives. After much discussion and many tears, we agreed that I'd move out, and we'd go to see a marriage counsellor.

The next difficult conversation was with my mum and my step-dad, Chas. Instead of support, all I got from Mum was, "What will people say? No one is divorced in our family."

I kept in touch with Dan and we met up after I had told Graham I was leaving. I didn't leave him for Dan, because he was also married. This is where some of you will judge me for being a family-breaker. This wasn't the case; Dan was a serial adulterer. He told me he had previously had several affairs, so either he was excellent at keeping them secret, or his wife knew and accepted it in her own way. I never contacted him at his home, and never left messages or anything that could be found, so it was his responsibility for what he did. We only met up a few times, as he lived in London. For me the best thing about the relationship apart from our friendship was that he proved to me that I wasn't frigid! We had a short but good relationship where we visited art galleries together and had other interesting outings aside from the sex.

In 1992, I moved into a furnished flat in a building on Eldorado Road, Cheltenham. I was the only woman in the house. All the other flats contained divorced or single mature men. Graham and I still had a joint account, so we continued to pay for all the house bills and now the flat too. We met up for the occasional night out together, though I was trying hard to create my own independent life after eighteen years of marriage. Graham was hoping I'd go back home.

So, here I was at forty and living on my own for the first time ever. Lots of friends supported me though, inviting me out for dinner or for weekends and generally being there for me, which was exactly what I needed. What I didn't know was that my single life was about to start, which was going to keep my work colleagues highly amused. They were all married and hadn't been on the dating scene for years. Things were about to change.

One of my younger teaching friends loved soul music and as un-PC as this may sound, had a 'thing' for black men. I also love soul music, and love dancing, so when she asked me to go clubbing with her I thought *Why not!*

Off we trotted to the club she had been told about. There was definite disappointment as there was hardly any soul music and the majority of the other clubbers were white, unsurprising, as at the time Cheltenham was a predominantly white town. It was actually the wrong club. The following weekend we found the club she had meant to go to, 'Gas'. The club was brilliant; a disco on the upper floor and in the basement a soul room. The club had a great reputation and people travelled there from Bristol, Birmingham, London, and even further afield. The clientele in the basement was an almost equal mix of black and white. Although some men were obviously there to chat the women up, people were also there to dance. Unlike the upper floor, where guys would suddenly start dancing with you without asking, in the basement they chatted to you away from the dance floor, and when you were on the floor it was all about dancing. There was no dancing around handbags either, that wasn't cool.

I loved the music and I was in my element *and* keeping fit without having to go to the gym! The biggest surprise was that one of the main DJs, known nationally in the soul fraternity, was my neighbour, Jerry Hipkiss.

On my third visit I was sitting down to have a drink to cool down when a handsome guy, KC, approached me. He asked me to dance and we spent the rest of the night dancing together. He asked if he could take me home. Suddenly my newfound confidence had a wobble. For all the years I hadn't dated, things had changed. Remember the 'only coffee' conversation? How on earth do you have that conversation without assuming that he wants more than *just* coffee, and without seeming a complete novice?! Somehow after trying to say 'no' to him coming back, I was persuaded that he would walk me home. We had coffee with extras, but no sex; I wasn't ready for that on the first date.

We arranged to see each other the next day. This meant me driving over to see him at his RAF quarters in Gloucester. I managed to ward him off for a couple of dates but, in the end I succumbed to his charms. It was definitely worth surrendering! When I got up the morning after, I noticed that KC was lying at a strange angle; the bed leg had fallen off. Obviously, the earth had moved!

Monday morning at work, I got a lot of teasing when I asked if anyone had a few spare bricks I could have to put under the bed!

KC loved music and he introduced me to a range of musicians I'd not heard of, so I gradually started to build up my CD collection of soul music. When I first met him, he was leaving the RAF, which I was pleased about; I've never wanted to go out with someone in the Armed Forces as there are too many issues that I have problems coming to terms with. He had been a gun instructor and had served during the Kuwait War.

Dating in the 90s was so different to when I first started. He didn't actually take me out anywhere; we would meet up at the club and then he would come back to mine, or I'd go over to his. It seemed, talking to the other girls at the club that this was the norm. I didn't feel that I completely got to know him though; he kept a lot of himself hidden and I know he had a temper that he had to keep under control. After a few months he went off to Catterick for his de-mob training.

Having been a bit of a nun in my teens and early twenties and remaining a virgin until marriage, I made up for it now. Whereas when I was young I was worried about what other people thought, and terrified of getting pregnant, now I had a new freedom. Dan, who I occasionally spoke to on the phone, had proved I was a sexual person, and now KC had fully unlocked that part of me. At the age I was, I didn't care what people thought, it was my life!

I met a lot of younger guys at Gas who were mostly Caribbean descent and about ten years younger than me. None of them seemed to have a problem with age either. I was the fittest I'd ever been and confident in how I looked and felt. Life really was beginning at forty!

1990-92 – Conrad

I was working as a mechanic in Birmingham, but it wasn't working out. So, one evening when the garage shut, I went back, got my tools and left. While working at the garage as a mechanic, a lot of guys who worked at Eurodollar, a car rental company, used to drop in. They had mentioned that the company were always looking for casual drivers. I went along and was taken on with starting pay of £2 an hour, which would now be classed as a zero hours contract these days. Working as a casual driver meant that I didn't have a regular area, so I could be sent to Leeds, Liverpool, Manchester, or London; basically, anywhere they needed vehicles delivering.

I enjoyed driving, and the reason I took on the casual work at such a low wage was that I knew that if I hung around and went in every day, there was always someone leaving, and I would have a chance of a full-time job. Determined and focused, I got up early every morning for a year until a full-time job did become available.

The other thing about working as a casual driver was that it was a great way to gain good driving experience, and learn to read maps well. As a new driver, I had to follow one of the full-time drivers when a vehicle was being delivered.

One day he said, "You're going to have to stop following me and learn how to read an A-Z if you want to get around."

Again, my determination set in, I went out and bought an A-Z, and studied it cover to cover, so that eventually I could turn to any page and find my way to the destination. There were no sat navs in 1992, you had to use your brain and a map.

Alongside the driving, we also had to valet the cars too. They were always brand-new vehicles, which also meant that I had the experience of driving a range of different makes of cars. If you worked late you could take the car home and bring it back the next day and you also got cheaper rates on rentals at weekends. This was handy, as I didn't own a car while I lived in Birmingham. With this job though, if I did want to go anywhere, I had access to cheap cars to rent.

1993 – Lis and Conrad

New Year, 1993. I couldn't have believed the changes that were going to take place in the coming year.

This was my first Christmas as a singleton, and

I preferred not to go to Mum's, but stay in the flat in Eldorado Road for Christmas and New Year, mostly with KC. Later in January, we spent our last weekend together before he left to go back home to Ipswich as his RAF career had ended.

A few weeks later in February, I was shocked when I missed a period. We had always used condoms, well apart from that once time. Surely, I wasn't pregnant? I was forty and I thought not at my most fertile. My periods were always on time, to the day.

After taking the pregnancy test my worst fear was confirmed. I was pregnant. My doctor, who I had only recently registered with, was a middle-class Cheltenham lady in every sense.

Her reaction to my request for a termination was, "You should leave it a few days to consider your options. At your age, you won't get the chance again."

I had considered it; every hour since finding out. My heart felt elation; for the first time I felt like a real woman. Although I had previously chosen not to have children, now hormones were surging through my body and affecting my emotions in unexpected ways. I was pregnant. I was a whole woman!

My head, on the other hand, was being pragmatic. The realities were: I was living in a rented flat; redundancy was a high likelihood, which would mean no regular income; and as for the father, KC, I was in lust with him not in love. Imagining my life at forty, taking into account all of the latter, and the fact that my baby would be mixed-race, yet another huge

129

issue to contend with, the decision was obvious to me.

KC was surprised when I gave him the news and told him what I was going to do. The surprise for him was that I'd not taken the morning-after pill. This is where my naivety kicked in. Having been married for eighteen years, I'd missed out on the minefield of sex and dating and I thought the morning-after pill was a joke. The joke was on me.

After the trip to my well-meaning doctor, I went to the Family Planning Centre. They were amazing, no judgemental comments. Instead, the lady doctor pointed out that I probably fell pregnant because I hadn't had sex for all my previous years of marriage, similar to Forces' wives who often fall pregnant when their husbands return after months away. Like my own doctor she also mentioned about this being my last chance but, when I explained my reasoning, she agreed.

I am continually grateful for living in a country where women have the choice to make decisions about their own bodies and ultimately their futures.

Dan and I were occasionally talking at this time, and when I told him what I was doing, as a Catholic, he was incredibly judgemental, which I found totally hypocritical. In his eyes it was okay to have affairs with people, and cheat on his wife. I wonder what would happen if any of his mistresses had become pregnant and called for his support.

Mothering Sunday, which was only a few weeks after my termination, was hard. Even though it had been my own choice, to be celebrating everything motherly was like some cruel payback. It was particularly difficult not being able to talk to Mum; it would have given her a heart attack.

Life continued and, after Graham and I sold our house in Down Ampney, I bought a modern new flat; the first place of my own. It was a one-bedroom flat within walking distance of Cheltenham centre and a few hundred yards from the railway station. My piano and harp took up a lot of space in the lounge/kitchen, but there was still room for a sofa bed and my computer. I bought myself all-new bedroom furniture, and was set up in my new home. My divorce was made final on 15th July, and I moved into my new flat the following day.

In June all of us remaining in the Arts advisory team were made redundant, which is why I had bought a small flat. I wanted to be sure I could afford everything. Before I left the team, the County Council paid for a word processing course as part of my redundancy package. This helped a great deal because as I could already touch-type I registered with a temp agency and did a small amount of temping.

Gloucester County started to pay me to lead training courses for them and I also began to get work around the South West and further afield. Gradually, my freelance work began to build, and I was able to live on those earnings alone.

Around this time another friend of mine, also working in music education, was approached to write a music scheme for a national, schools' publisher. She asked me to co-write the scheme with her, so we embarked on writing Nelson Music. I was glad I was living alone for this, because I found that I often had good ideas early in the morning and would get out of bed around 4am, write for several hours, and then go back to sleep. On other occasions, I'd write late into the night, but for either of these activities, the early or late writing didn't work so well if I had employment the next day.

Life was good: I had regular self-employed work; a great social life; I was enjoying being single; and I wasn't looking to get involved with anyone for a long-term relationship in the near future.

Nights out to Gas continued, and I had a new girlfriend, Lisa, who I'd met there. Despite the fact that I was the same age as her mother we got on surprisingly well. Either she was old for her years or I was a lot younger, or a combination of the two. Lisa lived with her parents, but at the weekends she was often out all night, with seemingly no consequences from her parents or intervention on their part. On Friday and Saturday evenings we'd be together, listening to music with a drink and getting ready go out to the club. Two of our favourite tracks were *Mr Wendal*, by Arrested Development, and Alexander O'Neal's, *Love Makes No Sense*.

One Saturday in August, Lisa and I were dancing when, in between the other dancers, I noticed this good-looking guy across the dance floor. He was wearing pale blue denim jeans and shirt and was an amazing dancer. I thought he might be one of the American airmen that frequented the club, because his dancing wasn't made up of the standard dance moves that a lot of the other guys had; he had a distinct style that I loved. I pointed him out to Lisa, who said she knew the other guy he was with. I disappeared off to the ladies, and when I came back, Lisa was on the dance floor, giving me a knowing smile!

To my amazement, the good-looking guy came up to me and said, "Your friend said you fancy me!"'

Not the most original chat-up line, but feeling like a sixteen-year-old, I said "Yes," and we went onto the dance floor together.

Conrad's recall of this event was that his cousin told him that Lisa, who he knew, had a friend who fancied him. Conrad thought they were playing a trick on him, because he loves dancing and he went to clubs to dance, not to pick up girls. Despite thinking this, he decided to ask me to dance. He maintains when I mention it that his poor chat-up line was actually a joke!

Either way, we had our dance and when the track finished went our separate ways. After the dance he was trying to decide what he wanted to do, thinking *Should I? Shouldn't I? Am I interested?...*

As he didn't ask me to dance again, I thought he had decided I was too old for him. We did, however, spend much of the night smiling across the dance floor at each other.

While Conrad was sitting with Evan trying to decide what to do, I (full of rum-induced courage) approached him to ask his name. After he told me, there was an awkward silence, and I was thinking, *just walk away*, when he asked me for my number. He said he'd ring me the next night at 5pm.

I couldn't believe it when he *did* ring me the next night at the allotted time. Most of the guys I'd met were flaky when it came to keeping promises; this was a huge improvement. We didn't have mobile phones in those days, so he had to put in some effort to make the call and go out to the phone box.

Thinking he was about twenty-three, I asked how old he was. Twenty-eight came the reply. I warned him that I was a little older than that. He thought I was thirty-something, which was great, and, even better, he wasn't worried when I told him my age.

I discovered that he lived in Birmingham and, along with his cousin Evan, they had come to Cheltenham for Evan's brother's twenty-fifth birthday party. The party wasn't going well, so they all decided to go to Gas.

We arranged for him to come down to my flat the following Friday. He hired a car from work and drove straight down to Cheltenham. He forgot about food and, on my part, I had stupidly assumed he'd eaten before coming. Around 9.30pm he suddenly asked if he could have something to eat! We chatted and laughed, talking about music, films, everything really, and got on so well, it was amazing.

He was impressed with my CD collection of soul music; he was still using cassettes. I felt so relaxed and comfortable with him in such a short time of meeting him. When it came time to sleep, having lost my shyness, I said he could either sleep on the settee or with me. Conrad said he hadn't dated for such a long time it took a little time for the penny to drop and realise I was inviting him to sleep *with* me! However, he made the right decision and we slept together.

I fell hook, line, and sinker for him that night. I knew Conrad was special. I'm a sucker for eyes, and he does have the most gentle, dark-brown eyes that made me melt… and have done so ever since.

He, on the other hand was, like a typical man, thinking, *Let's see where this goes*. He says that he was impressed with how much I liked music; that I liked the same films as him; that we laughed at the same things; and that he found me intelligent and multi-talented. I was totally going with my emotions, whereas he taking a more pragmatic approach.

That first night the thing that made me feel so amazing was that he held me as we went to sleep, and he gently rocked. I have always had the tendency to rock slightly as I go to sleep, which I put down to Dad gently rocking my bed when I was a toddler. Now here we were on our first date fitting together like a proverbial glove. Having spent years of sleeping separately from Graham, this was such a caring moment; I cherished it.

The next night we drove to a club in Handsworth called Bonds. Conrad had already arranged to go there with a friend from work, so he spent some of the night dancing with him and some other lads. I was perfectly happy dancing on my own. I could easily see where he was as he was wearing a scarf on his head – the only guy there doing so and managing to look great in it! During one track when a lot of the guys were jumping, I could see his scarf-adorned shadow dancing on the wall. It was a buzzing night and we drove back to Cheltenham in the early morning tired, but energised.

From then onwards we saw each other every weekend, either in Cheltenham or Birmingham. This was much to the surprise of Evan, who thought Conrad would have a fling and then move on. Unlike Evan, who was quite the ladies' man, Conrad wasn't interested in a fling.

The night we had been to Bonds, some of my other girlfriends were there too. One of them felt uncomfortable because, as white people, we were in the minority. I found her attitude hard to understand because to me I was having a fantastic night dancing in a room full of people doing exactly the same. It made me wonder if she ever considered that for most black people living in the UK whenever they are out and about and away from their own community, they are always in the minority, as are many other cultures. Maybe those people who complain about people seeking out their own community and living in cultural ghettos should ask themselves why? This was an argument I often heard growing up in Leicester. Is it any wonder people want to live where they feel comfortable and safe? English people do exactly the same thing when they live abroad; they often live within ex-pat enclaves.

The majority of Conrad's family do live in areas where there are other Caribbeans because they choose that comfort, and security, and enjoy being surrounded by others like themselves. Conrad has always been confident in himself to live anywhere. This doesn't mean that he has any negative thoughts about his Jamaican origins, he loves meeting and mixing with people from all cultures. He has always wanted to broaden his horizons.

Most weekends I would drive up to Birmingham and stay with Conrad in his flat because he had to work on many Saturdays. Rather than go out, because I hated driving in the city, I used to do his ironing. It's a chore that, sadly, I enjoy. He was surprised because, being self-sufficient, he wasn't used to anyone else doing it for him.

On Sundays, part of the routine was to take his clothes to the laundrette. One time while waiting, we were playing hangman. It was my turn to pick the word. Conrad kept throwing letters at me, with seemingly no order, so I asked him why he didn't give me a vowel. He didn't know what I meant. He didn't know about consonants either. I gently asked him some questions and then he shared with me that he had always had problems with learning. He said he felt comfortable telling me because I wasn't condescending but understanding and genuinely interested.

In the first year we were together, I used to worry a bit about the age difference between us, and that fact that I didn't want children. I had already told him about my termination, so when we had a conversation about children he said he wasn't desperate for them either and offered to have a vasectomy. As generous as that was, I couldn't agree to him doing that because he was too young, and at that point there was always the chance he may change his mind, so I was sterilised.

Over our years together, the lack of children has never been an issue for us, and never caused an argument. It did, however, cause a bit of disagreement with one of my friends. She surprised me when once in conversation she said that she would be extremely disappointed if her son were to go out with an older woman.

When I asked her why, her answer was, "Because it would stop me from being a grandmother". I asked her if she was interested in his happiness rather than hers. But, she stuck to her ideals.

Back in the nearly-exclusively-white Cheltenham, we continued to visit Gas. Once a month the club held a 'Soul Mine' which was frequented by soul music aficionados from far and wide. Later in the evening, as everyone else left, the jazz dancers took to the floor. These were predominantly men, including Oscar, who always travelled from Bristol with his crew. Oscar was for many years a regular extra in *Casualty*, and also a brilliant dancer. Only the good dancers dared to be out there on the dance floor; Conrad amongst them. I was proud of him and used to love the comments from the other women about how good my man was.

Near the end of one Soul Mine, a young lad was handing out tickets for a party at his house. We drove to the address in a sedate part of Regency Cheltenham and on knocking the door were told to go up to the top floor, but quietly, because his Grandma was sleeping. Silly really as the music coming from the top floor would have woken the dead! This was my first house party, and I had waited until I was forty and in Cheltenham – where had I been?

The top floor room had been emptied of furniture apart from some huge speakers that boomed out a bass that was begging to be answered by movement! A strong scent of weed was wafting around the room, so even without smoking you could almost inhale it.

All this was going well, when it seemed the doorbell rang; I say seemed, because we didn't hear it. Soon, though, we were looking out of the window at the police car parked outside. I was panicking, imagining the headline:

SCHOOLS ADVISER CAUGHT IN DRUGS RAID

Conrad and Evan were staring down in amazement at the police car, and the female and male officers. The music was turned off, and we could hear the WPC saying, "We've had a few complaints about the noise and wondered if you could turn it down please?"

Maybe Grandma wasn't sleeping so soundly… The music remained turned off, and we all obediently filed out of the house. Conrad and Evan were amazed by the civility of the whole affair. Had this been in Birmingham, a police riot-van with several burly officers would have turned up; not what they had just witnessed in refined Cheltenham.

The 1st December was Mum's eightieth birthday and I went alone to her celebration party; she wasn't yet ready for Conrad. However, we did drive up to see her and Chas on Christmas Day. I was dreading the visit, being aware of her old-fashioned views, including her previous comments that "Only a certain kind of woman goes out with a black man!"

Conrad, on the other hand, had been far more understanding and forgiving. He maintained it was all to do with her age and the generation she grew up with. He hadn't heard the conversation when I told her we were going to visit and she thought that Evan might be joining us.

"Well, I can only cope with one of them. I don't know what the neighbours will say."

As she handed Conrad his present she said, "I don't know if they have Christmas where you come from."

His answer was priceless; without missing a beat he said, "Yes, we do in Birmingham, thanks Rene."

After our visit she was impressed and thought Conrad very polite, honest and open. She also liked the fact that he sat holding her knitting yarn for her while she was winding the wool. Conrad generously also thought she was okay. I was glad to be back in Cheltenham ending the year with the new man in my life, who I was beginning to realise was someone very special. What a way to end a year that had seen me experience divorce, pregnancy, termination, redundancy, and moving house. More than enough excitement for one year.

1994-99 – Lis and Conrad

A year into our relationship and spending nearly every weekend together and on many of my holidays, I asked Conrad if he'd like to move in with me. I hoped it was something he would consider because of course it meant him getting a transfer with his job and yet again, leaving Birmingham.

He had been happy living there, and was happy in his job, so had never considered leaving until I suggested it. Also, he had never lived with anyone. But, after thinking about it, came to the realisation that he was ready for commitment. He liked Cheltenham and also thought he could easily spend time with me.

Before asking him I had thought long and hard about sharing my life with someone again after previously being married for so long. I hadn't intended settling down again so soon and was looking forward to some 'me time', but knew I wanted to spend as much time as I could with Conrad.

I had Mum to contend with. She rang me one to day to talk about Conrad. She said " I don't think he's our sort of person."

I answered, "Well, he is mine," and told her that I loved him so if she wasn't happy, then that was her problem. I slammed the phone down, put the answer phone on and burst into tears.

After a couple of days, she did ring me to apologise, after all I was her only child and she didn't want to lose me. Sadly, it had taken me to the age of forty to recognise that I had been too preoccupied with pleasing her. Even though I had a successful career in education I was constantly reminded how she had worked hard to get me where I was. Of course, I'm grateful for the sacrifices she made to keep working so that I could go to college, but I think I might have had *something* to do with my career progression and success.

Conrad's sister also wasn't too happy when he told her he was moving. He thinks now that at the time she felt a kind of resentment. After all, she had helped him leave London and obviously loved having him nearby. Dawn is a home-bird and likes the security of familiar people and things around her. Even several of the guys of West Indian descent who worked with him in Birmingham questioned why he was moving to an all-white area like Cheltenham, where they considered people to be snobs. But Conrad always felt comfortable in his own skin, wherever he has lived. He doesn't feel the need to be surrounded by people who look like him.

Physically, we are all defined by our colour, age, and visible differences that others feel they can judge. But we define ourselves by our identity; it's what makes us all unique. Brothers and sisters in the same family can define themselves completely differently;

British, Jamaican, Afro-Carribean, West Indian. It is up to each of us to take ownership of who we are, and for some that means remaining within the comfort and support of people with similar backgrounds.

Conrad knew it was time for a change and a move forward rather than continually looking back or staying still. Luckily, he managed to get a transfer to Gloucester and we were together.

The next few years were a time for us to settle in together and get used to each other's little foibles. It wasn't too difficult because we are both pretty easy-going. The hardest thing for both of us was emotion, in totally opposite ways. I cry when I'm happy or sad and sometimes both together which for Conrad who had spent most of his life feeling unable to share his emotions with anyone, was daunting. I'm of the school where you don't bottle things up inside but let them out. He didn't know how to un-bottle them at all. Whenever I cried he comforted me but almost at arm's length. He didn't actually say 'there, there' but he may as well have done.

The first occasion to test us was our first holiday together, which was nearly a disaster. I made a last-minute booking to Tossa Del Mar in Spain. We arrived at the resort late at night and it didn't look that bad, but in the cold light of day we weren't impressed. It was reminiscent of a prison camp, with turrets at each corner that could have easily housed machine guns! The resort had seen better days and was definitely somewhere you wouldn't choose to go to if you knew where you were choosing to go.

The next morning when we woke up Conrad was grumpy and uncommunicative, which I hate. I can't bear it when someone doesn't talk. I was actually thinking about how good Graham was at holidays. Had I made a big mistake? However, by the end of the first day after a walk around the old town walls and brightened by the sunshine, we were fine. The rest of the holiday was okay, but we vowed never to go there again and on our return home I started to plan the next year's holiday. We definitely weren't going on a last-minute booking again and not to Spain. Conrad, unlike me, hadn't been on many holidays, and certainly not with a partner. He found it hard to relax and had to learn how to enjoy the whole holiday concept.

By the time we went on our next holiday together Conrad was getting used to the idea. We went to Canada, which is where Graham had always said we'd go for our twenty-fifth wedding anniversary. We needn't have waited that long, we could have afforded it earlier. This was our first planned holiday together and was after only one year together, not twenty-five.

When we arrived in Canada there was a strike in the hospitality industry due to which we ended up in a 5-star hotel instead of the 4-star we had booked. There were no complaints in our quarter at all. Throughout our stay we took the chance to do as much as we could. We visited Quebec, Montreal, Ottawa, St Adele, and Toronto. During our time in Ottawa we were lucky enough to witness the most spectacular firework display, which was part of an ongoing competition. By the end of the holiday, we knew that this was just the start of our travels together.

Completely out of the blue, we received a letter from Cynthia's solicitor telling us she was selling the maisonette in Northolt. As Conrad's name was on the deeds, when it was sold he would receive half of the sale. Conrad informed the solicitor that he didn't want half because, as far as he was concerned, it was Cynthia's home, not his. Time went on, and then he had a very annoyed Cynthia on the phone accusing him of trying to steal her money, and that we should contact our solicitor. Without bothering our solicitor, we wrote back to hers saying we wanted nothing to do with any monies from the sale. When this was all sorted, and Cynthia had received her money, she redirected a bill for her telephone and cable connection to our address. We sent it back, with 'not known at this address' written on it. Maybe this was her idea of getting her own back for Conrad leaving all those years ago without telling her.

How Mum managed to actually verbalise the fact I was living in sin I don't know, as it must have rankled with her Puritan views. After we'd moved in together we went to visit her and Chas. Mum had told me several times that even though she knew we were sleeping together, she wasn't having 'any of that business' in her house! Even some of her friends had tried talking to her, but to no avail; she was adamant that we'd be in separate beds.

Funnily enough though, when we arrived we

were greeted at the door with "I've been much too tired over the last few days to make up two beds, so you can sleep together."

We had a surprisingly good time with them both, and Conrad and Chas got on like a house on fire. Mum had sayings for everything, which amused Conrad. When it was stormy she'd say, "It's looking black over Bill's Mum's." I never did know who Bill was. If you received a little less than you were expecting, she'd say, "It's better than a slap in the face with a wet kipper." Conrad uses the last one now, which always makes us laugh.

During the early part of 1995 I trained to become an OFSTED Inspector (Office for Standards in Education, Children's Services and Skills), which was some of the hardest training I have ever undergone. All of us potential inspectors were under scrutiny for the entire time of the course, including during the evenings when we had dinner. A few days into the training Chas suffered a stroke. Obviously, I wanted to leave to be with him and support Mum but I was in a dilemma. I had funded the course myself, which was expensive, and if I left midway through, I would have to re-sit the whole course again and I wouldn't get a refund. After talking to Mum, we decided that as I couldn't do anything practical to help, I'd stick out the course. As soon as the course finished I went over to see them both. Sadly, Chas died three weeks later so, once again, Mum was alone.

Despite some negative comments from a local

Inspector who thought I'd fail, I successfully qualified to become an OFSTED Inspector. This meant the opportunity of higher earnings in my self-employed career and gave me more authority. Inspecting schools was a great privilege. The team I regularly worked with had a fair Chief Inspector who was definitely not someone who believed in his own importance. Although we did visit a few mediocre schools many of them were good or excellent, with teachers who cared about their pupils educational and pastoral needs and it was a joy to watch some of those lessons. Most of the schools the team inspected were in the West Midlands.

I generally inspected art and music, and on one occasion had to inspect an art class that was taking place in the local church as part of joint Art and RE lessons. The class of primary children was made up of a wide cultural mix. The pupils were moving around the church either drawing or making notes about the different aspects of the building.

A young Muslim girl turned to me and pointed up to one of the stain glass windows and asked, "Do you know what that is?'" But without waiting for me to answer continued, "It's the Holy Ghost." She whispered to me with complete wonder and awe. Her display of respect for a religion that wasn't hers moved me to the point that, after replying to her, I had to turn away, as I could feel my eyes filling with tears.

Conrad's daddy, William, also died this year and, although he was unable to go over to the funeral in Jamaica, it was a great loss to him.

Moving to Cheltenham was a healthy move for Conrad. Like me, he had also suffered problems with his stomach. For years, he had suffered extreme stomach pains to the point where he was often bedridden and couldn't even keep water down. On several of these occasions he ended up in hospital. One such occasion was when I was staying with him in Birmingham and for the first time I witnessed just how much pain he was in. At this time he was so ill he ended up in hospital due to bad dehydration. When he joined my doctors' practice in Cheltenham, as part of his new patient-check he told them about this ongoing problem. Coincidentally an Australian doctor had recently discovered the Helicobacter Pylori virus, which they thought might be Conrad's problem. The virus has similar symptoms to an ulcer, so for many people it had never been diagnosed. After a series of antibiotics, he was, (and remains), completely cured.

Conrad couldn't believe it. He had suffered with this problem since the age of sixteen. It was brilliant for me too because for one, I hated seeing him suffer, but secondly it had been like going out with a teenage girl. He'd always leave something on his plate and ate small portions. Now, at last, he could eat normally and enjoy his food.

In May of 1996 I landed a job that was my dream position, Music Adviser for Wiltshire Schools. This meant that I had the responsibility for the curriculum music for all the schools, at all ages, in

Wiltshire. Another plus – I had a salary rather than relying on my self-employed income that was so liable to fluctuations. All the skills and experience I had gained previously as an advisory teacher and as a self-employed music consultant influenced my new role. I loved the job and worked with a fantastic group of other subject advisers, including Tom the science adviser, who has become one of my closest friends.

On Sundays we often got up a little late, especially if we had been out dancing the night before. The 31st August, 1997 was one such day. After getting up, I put the TV on and caught the end of a report about the death of someone royal. I assumed, due to her age, it was the Queen Mother who had passed away. I was incredibly shocked to hear it was Princess Di. Neither of us are big supporters of the Royal Family, but it is not something I would wish on anyone and it is always heart-breaking when someone dies young and so tragically. Like many around the country, we spent the day watching the news unfold.

After living in the flat for about five years and managing incredibly well in our limited living space, we had our first wobble.

One evening out of the blue Conrad suddenly said "I think I need to get my own place."

I was shocked. Wasn't he happy anymore? Had he stopped loving me? Was I so stupid and blind that I hadn't realised?

I asked "Don't you love me anymore?"

Instead of answering, he went quiet. This made

things worse for me and I started crying. As I mentioned earlier, any outpouring of emotion made Conrad uncomfortable, so he became even quieter. He wasn't used to expressing his feelings. He wanted to tell me that he loved me, but couldn't.

For the first time since being together, we went to bed that night without our normal cuddle; Conrad on one side of the bed with his back to me and me on the other, crying inconsolably. The next morning, he went off to work without even a "Goodbye".

With big puffy eyes, and looking very much like a frog, I rang my best friend Tom and told him that I thought Conrad was leaving me. Sensibly he told me to take the day off work. I rang another friend with whom I spent the day. During our conversation she mentioned, having worked with many people who were dyslexic, that often they can't find the words to express how they feel.

When Conrad came home from work we managed to talk and he was able to explain that he didn't want to leave me. He thought even though we were both paying for bills and the running of the flat, he should have his own place. His thinking was probably partly my fault. Previously I had said that I didn't want to buy anywhere with someone again. Having taken a backward step financially after my divorce I didn't want to do it again should a relationship fail. We talked though the things that were important to us and decided that we would ask our financial adviser Forrest to come and discuss what we could both afford. The idea was that we would each buy a small house and spend most of our time together in one of them. We went to sleep that night, completely together again.

When Forrest came to see us, after giving us advice about what we could afford, he said, "You two love each other, why don't you buy together?"

I spent the next day thinking about this. It would make more sense and I did love Conrad, so I should ignore my thoughts about splitting up and take a chance. Life is too short, and I didn't want to regret losing our time together. Conrad was pleased when I suggested it to him, so we started looking for our first house together. After selling the flat fairly quickly, we found a new-build in Hucclecote, Gloucester, and moved into our new house in December, 1998.

2000s –
World News

- 2000 world population: 6.102 billion
- Mad cow disease alarms Europe 2000
- Human genome deciphered and expected to revolutionise the practice of medicine 2000
- Y2K passes without serious failures 2000
- Foot and mouth crisis in UK 2001
- Almost 3,000 people killed in the 9/11 terrorist attacks on the twin towers in New York City, the Pentagon and in Pennsylvania 2001
- Queen Mother dies in her sleep aged 101 2002
- Saddam Hussein is captured by US troops 2003
- Concorde makes its last commercial flight 2003
- Use of mobile phones while driving is made illegal in the UK 2003
- An enormous tsunami devastates Southeast Asia on Boxing Day, killing 200,000 people 2004
- Seventieth anniversary of D-day commemorated in the UK and France 2004
- Pope John Paul II dies and Benedict XVI becomes the next Pope 2005
- London hit by Islamic terrorist bombings on 7th July, killing 52 and wounding about 700 people 2005

- Prince Charles marries Camilla Parker Bowles 2005
- YouTube goes online 2005
- Surgeons in France carry out first face transplant 2005
- Saddam Hussein convicted of crimes against humanity and hanged 2006
- Barack Obama is elected the 44th President of the US 2008
- British government introduces emergency legislation to temporarily nationalise Northern Rock due to the bank's financial crisis 2008
- Carol Ann Duffy is appointed as the first female poet laureate of the UK 2009

UK Prime Ministers

Tony Blair, 2000-07
Gordon Brown, 2007-10

2000-09 – Lis and Conrad

Working in Wiltshire and living in Gloucestershire meant that every Sunday night I left to stay with my friend Tom for at least three days of the week. I was finding it harder to leave Conrad each weekend. So, in 2001 we decided to move to Wiltshire and began our house hunt. This was much harder than we expected, as we hadn't realised how expensive houses were in Wiltshire compared to Gloucester.

Eventually we found a Victorian terraced house in Wootton Bassett and we moved in October. On our arrival the house felt damp and cold so rather than move my piano into that environment, I put it back into storage until we had rectified the problems. Our first night in the house was spent sleeping on the floor of the spare room. I was seriously regretting the move. Conrad's constant encouragement of 'I am marrying you in March' was meant to take my mind off the disappointment and look forward rather than backward. It worked.

Having previously moved to Cheltenham with me, now Conrad had moved yet again. Once more, he also had to change jobs. He found work as a courier with Reality, based in Swindon, although his delivery round was in Bristol.

We had now lived together for nearly ten years and more than anything I wanted to be Mrs McDermott. Conrad had never considered marriage, as only a few of his family had managed the state successfully. I wasn't a good advert for marriage either, albeit I had given it a good try. Jokingly, he started saying to me that he would marry me on my fiftieth birthday. Again, jokingly, he said, "You organise it and I'll be there."

My answer was to start organising it.

We decided on an extremely small wedding: two friends, Tom and Pan, and us. They travelled with us to Combermere Abbey in Whitchurch, Shropshire. On 8th March, 2002, wearing a musical '*I AM 50*' badge, I drove to our wedding. I had my makeup prepared professionally and didn't want to ruin it by falling asleep on the journey! Ours was one of the first weddings booked since the property had become a wedding venue. The beautiful building, which is a former monastery, has ten cottages in the grounds with cosy accommodation.

I told Mum we were getting married, to which her only comment was, "I'm glad you're not going to be living in sin anymore." No congratulatory comments or good wishes, but then I hadn't invited her. I thought it would have been a little hypocritical considering some of her previous comments about Conrad. Also, at the age of eighty-nine, she was finding it hard to travel and was a fussy eater. Conrad rang his brother and sister after the event to tell them. They were somewhat surprised.

On our return home we held the fiftieth birthday party, which was already organised, and revealed our marriage to our friends. It was lovely to share our happiness. After our marriage, for us, nothing was different, apart from the official 'stamp'.

When some people see Conrad and hear our surname, McDermott, they ask with incredulity, "Are you Irish?" We then have to explain that the majority of people descending from Caribbean origins have a slave-owner's surname. Slaves were given the surname of their owner. They had lost their identities when they were captured and enslaved, which is why it is so hard for Caribbeans to trace their ancestry.

Prior to meeting me, Conrad had only been on

holiday to Bournemouth when he was younger and then Jamaica in his teens. The latter had not been a holiday in the true sense as he had stayed with family and had never visited any of the main tourist venues on the island. During the next few years we travelled to many different places including Hong Kong, Bangkok, Italy on several occasions, Holland, and South Africa. After our initial bad experience in Spain, we did revisit the country and had wonderful time in Seville and Cadiz. Travelling with someone you love and want to share experiences with is the best way to see the world.

Our visit to South Africa was amazing. The strangest thing was to realise that only a few years earlier, we couldn't have travelled together or lodged at the same hotel due to the apartheid laws. Staying in Cape Town was a wonderful experience. When we stayed in Montagu for a short time, some of the local population, to whom the white South African's refer to as 'Cape coloured', were surprised to see Conrad and me together. To see interracial couples at that time was still a rarity.

Back in Cape Town, our friend Vince took us to visit some French nuns who worked in the community. They couldn't stop smiling when he introduced us as a married couple. Their happiness was a wonderful endorsement. We also visited Robben Island where Nelson Mandela had been imprisoned. It was an emotional trip and we both found it impossible to imagine the terrible conditions that the prisoners had to endure.

Apart from holiday travels, I was also extremely lucky to travel for my work on a few occasions. For several summers I took part in an international music course based in Finland. The Finns are fun-loving people and make you very welcome. Except for one musician from the US and our British entourage, all of the other attendees were from the other Scandinavian countries and Europe. Finland in the summer is beautiful, although with so many lakes, they do have a mosquito problem. The warm, balmy evenings melt into the day with little darkness between. We spent a lot of our evenings making music around a large fire, cooking sausages, and taking turns in the outdoor sauna. Absolute bliss! Through the magic of the web, and Facebook in particular, I manage to keep in touch with some of the Finns and the sole American.

My other work trips took me to Hong Kong. I love the vibrancy, hustle, and bustle of the city. My first trip was to deliver music training in a British school. After my week of work, Conrad, along with Tom and his mum, Betty, came out to join me. Tom had visited Hong Kong many times, and it was him that had referred me for the work. Having visited before, he was a brilliant guide. Before leaving the UK, Conrad drove over to Melksham to pick up Tom and Betty for the drive to the airport.

All was fine until they arrived. When Conrad got his case out and started to follow Tom and Betty, she asked, "Why is the taxi driver coming with us?"

She lived in the North East and, at nearly

seventy, hadn't met any black people. It hadn't crossed her mind he might be my partner. But, by the end of the holiday, Betty and Conrad were inseparable buddies. Sadly, Betty died recently, but pictures from this trip, including some with Conrad, appeared at her life celebration.

Tom, who is an excellent landscape photographer, bought a digital camera when they were first on sale in the UK. When he decided to upgrade I bought his old camera from him. The first time I took a picture with it was like magic. I was so excited that I could see the picture straight away. We were on one of our holidays in Italy and I went off on my own into the countryside photographing everything in sight.

I am a visual person and have always loved paintings and photography. However, I had never wanted to be involved with film where I had to develop the images in a darkroom. Firstly, whereas I have patience with people, I don't have it with objects and the thought of all the processes involved in creating a successful picture seemed rife with opportunities for impatience. Secondly, I thought it would be a mathematical procedure, and you know my feelings about maths. The digital camera was my saviour. This, although I didn't realise it at the time, was an introduction to my future career.

* * *

As with any of us who have elderly parents, it is a huge responsibility when they live miles away from you. If there are several siblings, then maybe you can take it in turns to visit. When you are an only child it is down to you and nobody else. At the age of eighty-nine, Mum lived alone in Cosby, Leicestershire. We had talked about her coming to live near us, but she wanted to remain close to her friends and the surroundings she knew. She had amazing neighbours who did her shopping, helped her with cleaning, and took her to any medical appointments she required. A lady helped her get ready in the mornings and then Mum managed to do most things herself during the rest of the day. Despite this array of helpful people, whenever I spoke to her on the phone she would complain she didn't see anyone. She was her own worst enemy, as she didn't like to go to any groups that were on offer, as in her words, they were full of old people.

Over time I become worried about her safety. Despite all of the help she was receiving, when cooking she frequently left the gas ring alight. If people did any shopping for her, she would offer to pay them, and having done this once she would forget and offer again. This is fine when the person is honest, but it would have been easy for someone to take advantage of her.

Eventually, and of her own volition she told me, "It might be time to go into a home."

She left this moment of clarity until the penultimate week of my school summer holidays. I drove over to Cosby and set off to visit some of the local care facilities for the elderly. It was a very depressing few days. Most of the homes were dull, and typically the ageing residents were sat around the edge of large rooms looking lost, staring vacantly at the walls. The other thing was that all of the homes had the smell of old people. There was a definite odour-de-urine as soon as you entered the building.

Eventually we discovered a brand-new care home that was opening in a village a few miles away. We both went to visit. This was a hotel by comparison. The facilities were excellent and the rooms were beautifully decorated in bright colours. The staff were friendly and helpful. And, it didn't smell because it was a new building. I arranged for Mum to have two weeks 'holiday' to see if she liked it.

Later in the day, back home at Mum's, one of her neighbours dropped by. Glaring at me in disgust Mum said, "She's putting me in a home."

I had to explain the reality of the situation then and for the rest of the week for any other visitors. After her two-week 'holiday' and much discussion, it was agreed that she would move into The Grange. Sorting out her house wasn't the upsetting job that I know many of my friends have experienced. This wasn't the house I'd grown up in, so it didn't hold memories of my childhood or Dad. I was able to feel detached. It was easier for Mum too. She was ensconced in her new home, so she didn't have to see her home being emptied out. She settled in with incredible ease, and was soon holding court, chatting away to all and sundry.

In December, after she went to The Grange, it was her ninetieth birthday. The staff were fantastic and provided us with a large room for her party. We invited a few close friends and she invited a few of the friends she had made over the past months. There were a few people she didn't want there, who decided to turn up anyway. With no thought of the offence she was causing, Mum looked straight at one of the poor ladies and shouted, "I don't want her here."

The situation was reminiscent of children who behave badly when someone they don't want to play with elbows their way into a game. The staff handled the situation perfectly and gently the unwanted guest was persuaded to leave.

Because the care home was new, many of the rooms remained empty, so Conrad and I were able to stay for a few days over Christmas 2003. It was an experience that I wouldn't like to repeat. We had to sleep in separate rooms opposite Mum's. At night she rang her buzzer so many times it was hard to sleep. I don't know how the other residents managed although, unlike me, they probably weren't feeling embarrassment. In the morning she would often moan about the bank nurses who were often of different ethnicities.

Luckily Conrad didn't hear when she said to me, "I don't like those black nurses that we get at night."

I don't think she actually disliked them at all. It was more likely that they didn't have a lot of patience with her due to the number of times she called them. Regardless, the staff held great affection for Mum. The number of staff working during the holiday season was fewer than usual. We helped out at meal times, pushing wheelchair-bound residents into the dining room and chatting to people who didn't get visitors. During this time Mum recognised what a genuinely kind person Conrad is. Sadly, it took until then for her to come to this judgement even when all of her friends enthusiastically accepted and liked him.

The following October, while leading a music workshop in Tewkesbury, I had a phone call to tell me Mum was in hospital. She'd had a severe chest infection, but the doctors couldn't give her the medication she required due to her other conditions. I felt completely useless being so far away and unable to down tools immediately. Mum had always been prone to illnesses that affected her breathing, including asthma. In her seventies she had been diagnosed with thrombocythemia (a condition that leads to abnormal blood clotting), which meant she had to take blood-thinning tablets.

The next morning, I drove up to Leicester to visit Mum and was horrified to see a pathetic old lady who was barely conscious. Up until then, and even though she was ninety, she was always lively and chatty. Now she looked like a shrivelled version of herself. She was so poorly I don't even know if she knew I was there. For the next few days I spent my time driving up and down the Fosse Way to Leicester. The last day I saw Mum she was complaining of her stomach hurting.

That night I had a call telling me that her bowel had split, which had caused septicaemia. The doctors didn't think she would survive an operation to rectify the bowel. She was too poorly for them to operate due to her asthma and chest infection. She didn't survive the septicaemia. On a rainy day in October 2004 Mum died before I could get to the hospital. Chas' son, my stepbrother and his wife were with her as she died, but her only child was absent.

When Conrad managed to get back from Bristol where he was working, we drove to Leicester. I didn't cry, not then. I went into organisation mode, as I had when Dad died. My stepbrother's wife kept telling me to go and see Mum. I didn't want to see her dead. The memory of my Grandad has always stayed with me. I wanted to remember Mum smiling, her eyes alive and laughing. I don't regret this decision, but I do feel guilty for not getting there in time to be with her when she left this world.

At the age of fifty-two I was an orphan. Suddenly, I felt alone and bereft. Although obviously I had Conrad, who was a huge comfort to me. My stepbrother is not and has never been part of my family. Had we grown up together as children it may have been different. He is purely the son of the lovely man Mum married. Having lost my dad when I was younger, and now losing Mum I felt more aware of my own mortality. It wasn't even as though I had a large extended family to turn to for support. Conrad was truly amazing in his understanding and ability to cope with my moods in moments of complete loss and grief.

In the year after Mum died, Conrad's birth-father, Frederick passed away. He felt sad, as you would for anyone who had died, but there was no father-son bond. Conrad didn't feel the emotion 'expected' at the loss of a parent. We attended Frederick's funeral, which was well-attended by many of his friends. Along with his half-brother, Conrad cleared Frederick's personal effects from his flat, the only thing he kept was his parents' wedding album. We think that, despite the divorce, Frederick must have kept Cynthia in his heart all those years, because he had cared for the album since 1964.

* * *

Literacy and numeracy had become the main focus of the curriculum to the extent that schools didn't have, or didn't want, to spend money on the Arts. My job was to support schools with their music curriculum. This meant as Music Adviser that I ran courses for teachers and supported them in their teaching. However, when I visited a school to give advice, they had to pay for my time, which meant that I had an earning target to meet each year. Due to these changes in curriculum and the lower number of schools buying my time, I wasn't hitting my target.

I was given extra responsibility as Key Stage 1 Assessment Adviser. I had been working alongside the assessment team already, but I wasn't confident about this new role. The job involved frequent trips to London to meetings with other advisers and the government-led body who put the assessment into place. Then I had to disseminate this information to head teachers and their staff. I also had to train school staff and the county group of monitors on the requirements for testing. As much as I loved working with teachers and colleagues, this wasn't why I had gone into education. I don't fundamentally agree with testing young children or, more importantly, the style of the testing. We do need to know that children understand what they learn but teaching for tests doesn't ensure this.

When, at my annual appraisal, I was informed that I was being put into 'informal incompetency' I was devastated. My whole working life to this point was about enabling people to make music. Conrad is the love of my life, and my job was my passion. I couldn't imagine doing anything else. I got into my car to drive home, and rang Tom rather than Conrad, because I worked with him, and knew he understood the system we worked within. He was angry, almost to the point of wanting to sort out my boss!

When I got home I was so upset, sobbing uncontrollably and unable to speak. Conrad thought I'd been attacked. I felt I had let myself down. I was a failure, and what else could I do? We had planned to go away with friends that weekend and, as it happened, it was the best thing.

After the crying came anger, and then during the time away, I calmed down and decided to fight back. When I returned to work I discovered there were a few other advisers in the same situation. One resigned, one spoke to their union, and I decided I'd stick to my guns, and jump through the hoops they had set for me. These hoops involved a plan that was supposed to help me raise my earnings.

At the end of the set period, I was thanked for my hard work and commitment. However, I still wasn't able to hit my target.

On reflection, I may have lost my way a little with work, but this was during the months following Mum's death. Mum had always been my support. Before meeting Conrad she was the one I would share exciting news with. She was the one who knew me best and, in return, I always knew I was wanted and needed. Working with teachers and pupils gave me a huge feeling of satisfaction and purpose. I was able to share a skill I had. The thought of losing my job was overpowering.

Alongside my day job, I was spending more time working on my photography skills. I photographed many of my friends and their children. One of my musician friends has a beautiful daughter, Natasha, who is a singer. She had previously had photos taken for her portfolio but didn't like any of them. I told her that she would be doing me a great favour if she would let me photograph her. Happily, she did. We were both equally delighted with the results and she used some of them for her portfolio, which gave me great confidence.

Around the same time, Conrad's niece Irene asked me to photograph her wedding.

"I can't afford an expensive photographer, and I don't care what you capture, because I know you'll get some good pictures. I want you to do it," she said with an unfounded confidence in me.

I had taken good photos of her little girl, but a wedding was completely different and a huge responsibility. I booked myself on a wedding photography course in the Peak District. The course was excellent, and I learned all the things I needed to know. I also learned that I needed a superior camera to the one I currently owned. Kindly, a local photographer shared his knowledge with me, and helped set me up with the equipment I needed to take portraits and shoot weddings.

Irene and Marcus' wedding went without a hitch from the point of view of photography. I used all the tips that I'd been given on the course, which included use of a tripod. This meant that when guests were trying to take their pictures, they couldn't get too close to me. Working with large numbers of children and teachers gave me an edge when it came to organising people for group pictures. The only thing I didn't have control over were the guests who kept asking to be in the photos. I had a list, and no one was getting into a photo group if they weren't on the list! I had a few stern looks from some of the Jamaican family friends who didn't know me, but I stuck to my guns.

Now I had a portfolio of wedding, portrait, and children's images that populated my new website and that in turn helped me get bookings and start earning for my photography work. My first paid wedding was Natasha the singer, which was a great success.

Gradually, my photography work was building up and I was taking on more and more weddings throughout the summer. Feeling more disheartened each day with the education system and the passion for my 'day job' beginning to wane, I began to dream about becoming a full-time photographer.

Both of us love films and around this time we used to go to the cinema regularly. We went to see the film *Closer*, starring Julia Roberts in the role of a photographer. At one point during the story she has an exhibition of her portraits. I thought; *I want to do that!* I could clearly imagine myself in the same position.

Later I talked to Conrad, asking him how he would feel if I resigned from my job. This meant giving up my regular, healthy salary. Also, I was the main earner of the two of us, so a change in career would mean a big change in our income.

Being the wonderfully supportive person he is, he said, "Do it! If we can't afford the house, we can move into a flat. We haven't got kids, so do it. Life's too short."

Although money is important to live, it isn't the thing that drives either of us. In 2008 at the age of fifty-six I resigned from my adviser's job and started my own photography business.

I had already built up the equipment needed to run my business with the help of some of the money Mum left me. Working from home also helped to keep costs down. The drawback is that you always have access to the computer, and if there is a great deal of editing, then it needs to be done, whatever the time of day. Also, taking on weddings meant that during the summer months in particular I was out several Saturdays in a row.

I photographed fifteen weddings in my first summer as a full-time photographer. Sharing one of the most important days of people's lives is a real privilege, and I loved every romantic minute of it. Unlike some photographers you talk to, I didn't find weddings particularly stressful. I would only photograph one wedding per weekend, and that couple were my main focus. It was important to me that they felt relaxed working with me, and generally I accomplished that.

When Conrad wasn't busy working, he accompanied me as my assistant. He carried my camera bag; made sure I didn't leave any equipment anywhere; held the bride's bouquet during their shoot; and helped organise people for group shots. We were a team and people would comment positively on our work.

Often, after seeing us work with the couple, wedding guests would ask how long we'd been their friends. I used to be amused though, because wedding guests rarely realised we were married. One such occasion was a Jamaican wedding in Birmingham. The two female videographers took a liking to Conrad and spent the whole afternoon chatting him up. When we sat down for the meal, they were seated next to us. Conrad asked me about something on the menu. They were shocked that we were a couple. That option obviously hadn't crossed their minds.

Photography has given me many opportunities to meet people who I wouldn't have otherwise met. I managed to photograph two royals: Prince Charles at the opening of a local old people's home; and the Duchess of Wessex at Gloucester Cathedral for an event. Every day is different and I get to meet lots of new people, which I always enjoy.

Conrad was still working as a courier and he was out all hours. He worked long days from 7am, until around 7pm, and sometimes later. He also worked most Saturdays. On special days such as Mothering Sunday, Father's Day, Valentine's Day, Christmas Eve, New Year's Eve, he was often out delivering until late, not getting home until well after 9pm. His working pattern couldn't have been more different in every way to mine. Working for myself, I have control of working times and days that I work. Our rare, free weekends became a time to relax, watch films and listen to music.

The main danger I thought Conrad might encounter while working as a courier was a traffic accident. Something I'd never considered, until hearing his stories was that you put yourself in serious danger every time you deliver to a house where there is a dog. There are some lovely, cuddly, sweet dogs out there, but on several occasions your limbs are at threat when the dog owner is irresponsible. There were several moments where Conrad had interesting altercations.

He knocked on the door of one house and could hear a dog whimpering. His instincts were telling him to stay behind the gate but, for some reason, he didn't. As soon as the house owner opened the door, the dog jumped up and bit into his trousers creating a hole and missing the family jewels by inches, (which is why he always wore two pairs of trousers).

The lady said "He's never done that before."

If Conrad had a pound every time someone says that!

Several houses on his round were of the style where there is no access to park at the front, so you have to walk round from the back to the front door. The occupant of one such house, who was an elderly lady, owned an old Alsatian. Conrad rang the bell, the lady opened her door, and the dog started to chase him. He sprinted like Usain Bolt but the dog did catch up and bit Conrad on the arm. This entailed a trip to the A&E for a tetanus jab.

One winter night, around 7pm, he was delivering a 50-inch TV. The customer opened her front door and her two, large, St Bernard dogs started running through the porch towards him. His first reaction was to close the porch door, which meant dropping the TV. Instead of complaining about her TV, or asking Conrad if he was okay she yelled, "Don't you close the door on my dogs like that!" Unsurprisingly, he had a few choice words with her.

Whenever Conrad heard a dog barking when working it made him nervous. However, although it makes sense that dogs are protecting their territory, dog owners need to think about the safety of callers, especially when they are expecting a delivery.

It wasn't always irresponsible owners; sometimes it was an unexpected situation. Conrad was delivering to a house that had a long drive surrounded by a massive area of land. After parking his van, he walked towards the front door, warily looking around for dogs. All clear! The area around the front door had a three-foot-high picket fence, which Conrad climbed over to deliver his parcel. Having successfully done so he turned around to be confronted by two dogs. The larger of the two was a Rottweiler. Looking at his van in what now seemed the far distance, he thought, *That's it! What do I do now? How do I get out of this?'* He couldn't stand around all day and hope the dogs would disappear as he had loads of other deliveries. Then he saw his saving grace, a ball. He picked it up and, smiling at the little dog, he called, "Come on boy, fetch."

Conrad tossed the ball, and the little dog chased after it and eagerly brought it back to him in anticipation of another throw. This game went on for a short time under the continual glare of the Rottweiler. With each throw Conrad slowly moved back towards the picket fence, which he eventually managed to climb over. The little dog brought the ball back one last time and Conrad threw it and hastily got into his van.

Dogs aren't the only vicious creatures out there...

As he posted a calling card through the letterbox, something on the inside of the house made a savage stab at both the door and Conrad's hand.

Carefully he opened up the letterbox with his pen and was confronted by two, large eyes. The guard on the other side of the door was a cat – its claws drawn, ready to catch any unsuspecting person daring to deliver to his house!

2010s –
World News

- 2010 world population: 6.8 billion
- Thirty-three Chilean miners are trapped for sixty-eight days in a mine, half a mile underground. All are rescued safely 2010
- Kate Middleton marries Prince William 2011
- Japan hit by an enormous earthquake that triggers a deadly 23 foot tsunami in the country's north 2011
- Gary Dobson and David Norris jailed for life for the murder of Stephen Lawrence nineteen years after his death
- Malala Housafzai, a fourteen year-old school girl is shot by Taliban members. Targeted for her outspokenness against the Taliban and her determination to get an education 2012
- Queen Elizabeth II celebrates her Diamond Jubilee 2012
- London hosts the 2012 Olympic Games 2012
- Same sex marriage becomes legal in England and Wales 2013
- Duchess of Cambridge gives birth to Prince George of Cambridge 2013
- Edward Snowden leaks information about US top secret surveillance activities 2013

- British physicist Peter Higgs is awarded the Nobel Prize in Physics for his theory of the Higgs boson 2013
- Scottish voters opt to remain part of the UK in an independence referendum 2014
- Ebola outbreak in West Africa is worst since the virus was first identified almost forty years ago 2014
- Duchess of Cambridge gives birth to a girl, Princess Charlotte Elizabeth Diana 2015
- Immigration crisis continues as people flee from Syria, Afghanistan, Iraq and other war-torn countries to find new lives in the West 2015
- New pre-human species is revealed called *Hommo naledi* 2015

UK Prime Ministers

Gordon Brown, 2007-10
David Cameron, 2010-16
Theresa May, 2016-

2010 – Lis and Conrad

In 2007, due to the maintenance of RAF Brize Norton, the bodies of British Armed Forces servicemen and women who had lost their lives in Iraq and Afghanistan were returned home to RAF Lyneham. As the bodies were driven to the John

Radcliffe Hospital in Oxford to be received by their families, the cortège passed along Wootton Bassett High Street.

I remember how Dad always paused to stop in the street and removed his trilby hat in respect whenever a hearse was driven past. The members of the British Legion in town were of a similar generation and mindset and when they heard about these last journeys, they lined the street to pay their respect to the fallen soldiers. Over time more locals joined them, and eventually hundreds and sometimes thousands of people lined the High Street in silent memorial.

On one occasion, six bodies were brought through the town in the early evening. I had never been present at a repatriation, but this time, we left our meeting and took our place alongside the other people to pay our respects as the cortège passed. Normally standing on the High Street, you can hear the noise of traffic, people talking, children shouting, and, in the distance, the rumble of the M4. As we waited the cortège came into sight, the funeral conductor walking in elegant reverence at the front of the procession of six hearses. An eerie silence fell over the High Street and all of the natural sounds disappeared and I felt as though we were all holding our breath. Once the cortège passed, the noise returned, but we remained in our own silence for a time. It was one of the most moving experiences I've had.

Even after RAF Brize Norton was repaired the

decision was made to continue using RAF Lyneham for the transfer because of the huge demonstration of support shown by the people of Wootton Bassett. David Cameron announced in March 2011, "Her Majesty has agreed to confer the title 'Royal' upon the town, as an enduring symbol of the nation's admiration and gratitude". Our town officially became Royal on 16th October 2011, when Princess Anne brought the official letters patent to the Town Council. We were the only English town to be granted the royal title since 1909 and one of only three to be so honoured, the other two being Royal Leamington Spa and Royal Tunbridge Wells.

I was proud to be one of the several photographers working that day for the Town Council, along with all the national media who turned up in droves. My patch was the street; capturing the crowds. Others photographed from within the media compound. The RAF photographer was inside the VIP tent and another photographer with Princess Anne as she met local dignitaries and others amongst the crowd.

The High Street was full of TV crews setting up their equipment alongside the youth corps of the different Armed Forces who were marshalling the public. Due to the huge number of people expected and because the road had been cordoned off, I knew everyone would be crammed into the small pavements either side of the street. Although the event wasn't due to start much later, Conrad and I found our spot around 8am. It was a good move. Once the crowds arrived it was impossible to move even a finger. It was a huge privilege and exciting to know that the images I took on that day captured part of the history of the town, and will remain in the local council archives for years to come.

＊＊

Photographing wedding ceremonies often brought out the romantic in me, especially when I had Conrad with me. With our tenth wedding anniversary, and my sixtieth birthday approaching, I hatched a plan. Because our wedding had been a small affair, I decided it would be lovely to have a slightly bigger event for these celebrations.

We loved planning the event, but the hardest part was deciding who we would invite. Money constraints meant we could only afford a certain number of people, so we had to make hard choices.

On 10th March 2012, along with twenty friends, we held our party in a private dining room at the Cotswold Water Park Hotel near Cirencester. Several friends travelled from afar and stayed in the hotel, arriving mid-afternoon; the merriment started early. All the ladies had the opportunity to wear long dresses, and the men had the choice of whether or not to wear a tie, but were asked to wear jackets. One of our friends, who is the most amazing musician, wrote a song for us, "Say it Anyway", that he performed before the meal. It is not every day this happens but it is incredibly special to have a song written especially for you, and sung by the composer our friend, Bob Heath. My best friend Norman (from my college days) and his wife, Marikje, managed to make the party, even though the day before he had just arrived back from Nigeria. A month later we were unable to travel up to Lincoln for his party due to extreme weather. Typical!

Amongst other friends were Conrad's niece and her husband, and Tom who had been at our wedding.

Chris and his wife Sharon, who had attended the same training course as me, were in attendance, he as both friend and photographer. He captured the event, leaving us with some beautiful images from the day. Conrad, who had been far more nervous when we had married, gave a small speech, as did I. It was a day to remember, filled with joy.

For over a year in advance, Conrad had known he was going to be made redundant and was marking time until his job came to an end in May 2012. When he was eventually made redundant, his initial response was to look for a job immediately, and it took some persuasion from me to get him to relax for a few weeks. After all he had received a good redundancy package and had worked ridiculous hours for the past eleven years.

One of our acquaintances who is an actor, suggested to Conrad he apply to an agency to become an extra. He has always wanted to be involved in TV or film, so followed our friend's advice. We both took a week off work for our celebrations in March and during that time we travelled to Cardiff where Conrad interviewed for an acting agency. He was successful and over the next few months, while winding down in his job, got work as an extra on *Casualty*, and *Trollied*. He absolutely loved it and was in his element. While on set, Conrad bumped into Oscar, (a longstanding extra on *Casualty*) who had also been a regular at the Soul Mines at Gas, back in our Cheltenham days. Although both he and Oscar had frequently been on the dance floor during the jazz sessions (where the good male dancers had the opportunity to shine), they had never had time to converse. During the breaks in filming they now had time to catch up and talk about music. When we knew the programmes were to be aired we sat excitedly in front of the television. Our excitement was a little dampened. On one episode, we saw Conrad's feet, on another the blur of his jumper as he passed the camera. The best shot of him was getting into a taxi in the background with his arm in a sling.

For some time, we had wanted to move from our Victorian terrace into something more modern but didn't think we would be able to obtain a mortgage, due to my self-employed status. By this time, Conrad had made the decision, if we wanted to move, he needed a full-time job. He went to one of the recruitment agencies in Swindon where he had previously made deliveries. The ladies there found him a position straight away as a driver for a large builders merchant.

Sadly, because the acting agency tended to phone up to book him only a day or two in advance of a shoot, he chose to give up acting and concentrate on regular work. Eventually, the builders merchant offered him a full-time position working in the warehouse, which is where he currently works. Despite the change and his initial apprehension, he loves it. Unlike his latter-years as a courier, he is home by 5.30pm each evening, and doesn't have to work every weekend. We have our life back, and occasionally even manage to go away for long weekends.

Due to all of Conrad's hard work of the previous years, plus his redundancy money and some money I'd also come into, we realised we might be able to move after all. We started house-hunting in the summer of 2012 and found the modern house we had dreamed about. The move was only about a mile away from where we lived in Royal Wootton Bassett.

Our new house is a new-build, so we were able to choose all the fittings. Conrad had a saying, 'What Lis wants, Lis gets', which was funny… but true. I felt extremely spoilt. We chose all-new furniture, as none of our old pieces would fit in the much smaller rooms. Although the actual footprint of the house is much smaller, we have more rooms in the new house, including two bathrooms and a further toilet. This is just what we needed. The Victorian house had one bathroom, which included the toilet. Not too practical when you both simultaneously need the loo and have ageing bladders.

Having reached the age of sixty I also started to receive my teachers' pension. This meant we were able to use some of the lump sum to have an extra-special holiday. Several years ago, we met a lovely Japanese couple, Nao and Yayoi, who temporarily lived in Swindon with their two daughters. Since our meeting they had returned home to Tokyo, but whenever Nao came back for work purposes, he dropped in to see us. His last visit had been in March

2012, around the time of our celebrations. We told him we were planning a good holiday, so he jokingly suggested we should go to Japan. Japan is somewhere both of us have always wanted to visit. We found a good holiday specialist who planned our bespoke trip for us. The company enquired about our interests and places we wanted to visit, and then planned an itinerary. Our holiday was during the first two weeks of April 2013. Everything was booked for us in advance; our hotels, train tickets, special excursions, and even restaurants. This was absolutely perfect for us visiting a country with such a different language and culture to our own.

On the day after our arrival we met up with Nao and his family. We spent a wonderful day with them in Asakusa, an area of Tokyo. Since our last meeting they had another girl, Iori, bringing their family to five. The other girls are Hiyori and Yurari. It felt emotional when we had to leave them, and sadly we haven't seen them since, but we keep in touch. Each year we receive a New Year card, which includes a picture of the growing girls.

Japan is an exceptional place to visit. Cherry blossom season is generally in April, but as it is dependent on the weather, you can't be sure. This was something I had particularly wanted to see and travelling when we did, we were lucky enough to catch the end of the season. Wherever we went there were swathes of pink and white blossom. At times the blossom-covered streets look like snow.

The majority of our travel was by either underground, local, or bullet train (Shinkansen), the latter being incredibly comfortable and with far more legroom than our trains. During our tour we visited Tokyo then onto Matsamoto specifically to visit a typical Japanese castle and a village kept in its original traditional style. From there, we travelled through the Japanese Alps to Kanazawa, a particularly cultural city. We spent time walking around the old geisha and samurai districts. We also visited one of the most famous gardens in Japan, Kenrokuen. We took an early-evening walk and found the gardens full of Japanese families also out together to celebrate the time of the cherry blossom. The Japanese say that cherry blossom is like life, here for a short time and then gone.

Next, we travelled to the old capital, Kyoto. During our stay there we were extraordinarily lucky to spend time in a Japanese home, where the lady dressed us both in traditional costume. On our arrival we were presented with green tea and cherry blossom cakes. We then had a choice of different outfits. Mine was made of a beautiful pink, flowered material, and Conrad wore a short, grey, kimono-style jacket, with the most incredible silk design on the inside, rather than showing on the outside. It was explained to us that this was due to the world financial crisis in 2008. People didn't want to appear too ostentatious but still wanted to incorporate beautiful silk work in their clothes.

I don't know how ladies manage to walk and move so effortlessly when wearing a kimono, as the amount of material makes them extremely heavy. Underneath the main kimono, you have several layers of undergarments and you are tied into each layer. I couldn't even sit down in mine! We both felt magnificent in our traditional clothes as our hosts walked us down to the local temple. The neighbours appeared to be delighted we had chosen to wear their national dress.

The same day we were fortunate to find that the Imperial Palace was open to the public, which it seems, is a rarity. Along with several hundred Japanese tourists, we were able to walk around the gardens and look into some of the rooms.

One evening while in Kyoto we were taken on a walk around the geisha district (Gion) to catch sight of the geisha as they set out to work in the tearooms. The girls walked fast, which meant trying to take a good photo wasn't the easiest in the dying light. Geisha, historically are Japanese hostesses trained to entertain men with conversation, music, and dance. They wear traditional costume and makeup. Some people mistakenly think they are prostitutes, but this is wrong. They have to study hard to learn the ancient arts of music and dance. Businesses who are linked to particular Gion, or geisha houses, display a lantern containing that particular Gion's sign outside. So, you can tell by the specific pattern on the lantern hanging outside which Gion that accountant, dressmaker, shoe shop, or other business works with.

Our last stop before returning to Tokyo was Miyajima Island, situated in an inland sea, just off the coast from Hiroshima. Miyajima is one of the most beautiful places we visited, and we would have loved to stay there longer; it was so relaxing. What also made the visit special was staying in a Ryokan. This is a traditional, usually family-run hotel. The rooms have futon mattresses (a thick mattress which is laid directly on the floor for you to sleep on) with tatami floors (straw flooring).

Our hostess served the meals, which were incredible, in the traditional Kaiseki manner. The nearest equivalent in the UK would be a 'taster' menu, however this was so much better. Each course was explained and presented beautifully.

We visited the Peace Museum and Memorial in Hiroshima, which although I wasn't sure I wanted to visit, was moving to the point of heart-breaking. I also learned how much of my historical knowledge is sadly lacking. I always thought the atomic bomb dropped on Hiroshima was planned solely by the Americans. However, during our visit to the museum (and subsequent research on our return) we found out there had been cooperation between Britain and America in the development of nuclear weapons that ultimately led to the dropping of the bomb, and the resulting devastation it caused.

Unlike my visits to Hong Kong, where the Chinese stare at you, the Japanese don't. I don't find the Chinese rude; I think they are merely fascinated by our size. The Japanese would find it disrespectful to stare. They are an honourable and generous people, who went out of their way to be helpful. We will certainly go back when we can.

***

In May 2014 we visited Berlin for a short break. It was particularly fascinating for me to freely enter the parts of East Berlin that had been imprisoned behind the wall when I had visited in 1969.

The site where Check Point Charlie was is now a huge tourist attraction. This seems completely the wrong description, but by comparison to its past this is how it appears. Tourists from around the world flock to the area, where actors now man the barriers ready for photos, for a fee. The various museums give you an insight into the personal tragedies of the families, who overnight were split apart, and their sometimes bizarre escape attempts and incredibly harrowing flights to freedom.

Our hotel was situated in what had been East Berlin. It was interesting to see the new developments springing up and the old, grey, blocky communist buildings, creatively rejuvenated.

On our return home I held a launch party for my first published book about photography, *Headshot Diva*. It had taken me some time to feel confident enough to write it. My initial feeling was that other, more experienced photographers would be thinking 'who does she think she is?' In reality, the book is not for photographers, but for business people. My publisher, and now friend, David Norrington gave me great advice, support, and encouragement to go ahead and publish.

I had previously only been to one other book launch and had decided I wanted something a little different. Together with David I planned mine like a business network event, with extra celebrations. Everyone who attended was involved in a raffle and business owners who had contributed a prize were photographed with the winner, thus giving them photographs to use on their social media. There was a short quiz that entailed everyone having to find the answers in the book; a great way to engage them in at least flicking through the sections. We even had a cake with edible photos, which meant people could choose to eat bits of themselves or others, which caused some amusement.

There was one other person who I would love to have shared the book launch with; my photographer friend, Chris. He was too ill to attend after being diagnosed a few months before with lung cancer. His illness escalated quickly, and sadly he died on 29th June, aged forty-six. We had met on a year-long training course several years before, that both he and his wife Sharon were attending. This is the same Chris who had photographed our big celebration in 2012. He was a lovely, bubbly man who was always ready to laugh and a great photographer to boot. Chris had helped me photograph the large wedding of an African couple, which gave us the opportunity to capture some truly beautiful and unique images. He was fun to work with and easy-going, which was needed at this particular wedding, as it was a demanding and hectic day. Although we didn't see each other often, every couple of weeks we'd chat on the phone, something I miss. Chris was someone once met, you never forget.

Alongside Chris, there are three other people who have been instrumental in my photographic development. Tom, as I mentioned, is the person who introduced me to digital photography and initially encouraged me to take photos.

The next person is Simon Watkinson of the Peak District Photography Centre. I attended some of his courses when I was first asked to photograph a wedding. His workshop was invaluable. As was his advice about buying a more professional camera.

Last but not least, Damien Lovegrove. It was Damien's course 'Evolve' where I met Chris and Sharon, amongst others. Damien's course set me on the path as a professional photographer. He gave us all the tools and information we needed to run a business, alongside the technical knowhow. One of the best outcomes of the course, alongside the photography, were the friendships made during the year.

* * *

A happy event of 2014 was Conrad's fiftieth birthday. He didn't want a party or a big celebration, so instead I asked him if he'd like to go somewhere special. His choice: Cheltenham.

We had a fabulous two-night stay at the Queens Hotel in the centre of the town. Our room had a fantastic view towards Montpellier, the main street. His celebrations started with a champagne cream tea, followed by meals in two of our favourite restaurants on each night of our stay.

During the second day, Glenn, one of my local photography friends arranged to take photos of the two of us. It makes a change for me to be on the other side of the lens, and Glenn was brilliant. He soon had us posing in the hotel and in some of the gardens around the town. The cover picture of this book was taken during that day in our hotel room.

The dragon tattoos were a new addition for both of us. On New Year's Day, many years before, we had talked about having tattoos. It had taken over ten years to get around to it, but this year we both took the plunge. Me, being a complete scaredy-cat made Conrad go first. I wanted to see how painful it was, but it wasn't as bad as I'd expected.

Why dragons? We were both born in the year of the dragon according to the Chinese zodiac calendar. There are twelve animals representing the cycle of years. Because our age gap is twelve years, we have the same animal. The Chinese believe you are blessed to be born in this particular year.

Our tattoos are based on dragons we bought while in Hong Kong. Conrad's is a copy of a brass dragon and mine of a gold-leaf picture.

Having read Stieg Larsson's book, *The Girl with the Dragon Tattoo*, and discovering the heroine is my namesake, I'm particularly amused that I can now have the same title. Obviously a little far-fetched at my age referring to myself as a girl, but I can dream…

After three previous trips to Jamaica, (once when he was eighteen, once in his thirties, and lastly in his forties), we took a trip there together in May 2015. For this one and only time he didn't stay with family. He chose to take me to a beautiful hotel in Montego Bay. On the other visits he had spent time with family and never visited any of the island's tourist attractions. He was adamant that on this occasion we would take opportunities to see as much as we could.

For the first time Conrad snorkelled from the deck of a catamaran; watched the sunset from Rick's Cafe in Negril; climbed Dunn's River Falls in Ocho Rios; and swam with dolphins. He had the time of his life and enjoyed every minute.

However, the main reason for going to Jamaica was to visit Mummy, who we may not get the chance to see again, as she is in her late eighties, and not in the best of health. Sadly, due to family disagreements, we didn't get to see her, and I didn't get to meet her, which I was looking forward to. Despite this, I think deep down Conrad had pre-empted this scenario in his mind and didn't let it ruin his holiday.

Writing this book has made me recall so many people and events. Some people you meet through life come and go naturally without any great loss. Others I've lost touch with who I miss, and often wonder about them and their lives.

At college in Manchester I was close friends with a girl called Ruth. She attended my wedding to Graham, and then we completely lost contact. For years I used to dream about her, and the fact I failed so miserably to find her often upset me. Some years ago, I became resigned to the fact that I'll probably never know where she is.

Recently, I contacted another friend from college, who I last saw in the 80s. Again, for a long time after losing touch, I tried to find him to no avail. Then, last year, not for the first time, I typed his name into Google. Incredibly, and to my great shock there he was. Denis. I emailed him and got a response entitled 'Here I am'. In his replying message he said "My ghast has never been so flabbered!", which I remember is so his humour. When we met in London, and as I stood waiting for him, I was recalling his infectious laugh. I suddenly heard it, and there he was, some thirty years later; the same Denis I remembered. We spent a wonderful afternoon together catching up on decades. Last May, Conrad and I took a trip to the capital for a week, and we met up with Denis and his husband, Paul. We are now in touch regularly and it's like we picked up where we left off in the 80s. True friendship stands the test of time and change.

As youngsters we tend to define more mature people as 'old' just by their numbers of years lived and their physical appearance. Of course, our looks change but inside we are generally the same people we were when we were much younger. We may be more experienced, more knowledgeable and struck by sadness and loss, but our real essence remains the same. This is what you recognise when you see a friend after so many years and instantly connect with. Conrad always says to me that he doesn't see my age. He sees the 'me' inside. The 'me' that makes him laugh, surprises him, makes him proud, and the woman he loves; not the fact I'm in my sixties!

* * *

Friday 24th June 2016, was a hugely disappointing day for us. Both of us were upset and surprised by the Brexit result, but personally I felt as though I was

191

grieving and in many ways I was. I have never lived in a time when I felt the country was so divided.

Conrad was too young to vote when we joined the EU, whereas, at the age of twenty-one, I voted 'yes'. We are part of Europe, geographically, and to us it seems sensible to remain and work to make changes from within, rather than try to go it alone on the outside. However, we both recognise some peoples' need to take charge of our own laws and governance. What did upset us was the spate of racist attacks and rants by people who suddenly seemed to think it appropriate. Overnight people already living and working here from the EU were suddenly made to feel unwelcome in the country they call their own. I love living in a country where we accept people for their different cultures and beliefs and I think that this adds to the richness of Britain. To accept people for who they are, whatever colour or creed, is a fundamental belief of mine. This is why I was so upset by what I hope is a minority of people who voted for Brexit because they want to oust people who aren't British. We need to be aware of the numbers of people entering the country due to practicalities such as housing, schools, and health provision, but not because immigrants are taking our jobs. Unless there are extenuating circumstances, everyone has access to job vacancies if they really want to work. Without the many people who came here as immigrants much of our infrastructure would not be working as well as it is. Take a close look at the NHS and transport workers, many of whom are people who we invited here to help us out when our country needed them.

Brexit will happen, but we, as people need to make sure it's done with compassion.

Coincidentally, several months before the Brexit vote was even mooted, after talking to friends who had undertaken the same process, we decided to have our DNA traced through an online service. It only gives you a broad view on your background, but for Conrad, as a descendant of slavery, we thought it would be an interesting exercise.

When the results came through unsurprisingly Conrad's DNA is 91% African. The 91% is split across 11 African countries. The other 9% of DNA traces back to Europe. What we did find interesting though is that there is no mention of Jamaica. My own results showed that I'm 100% European, with 60% Great Britain and the rest from Ireland, Western Europe, the Iberian Peninsula, Italy, and Greece. Given my name, I was very disappointed to find I had no Scandinavian DNA, especially as Conrad has 1%! I'm not sure that we will do much with this information at the moment, but maybe when we're retired we might look into it more. It was however, a very interesting process to undertake.

2017 – Lis and Conrad

The old lady stopped in her tracks and stared from one to the other. A good look at him; a good look at her, and back again. They may as well have been aliens by the effect they seem to have on her...

This is what Conrad calls the barcode look, when people look from one of us to the other and

193

back again, several times. We also have the lingering open-mouth-stare look and the Colonel Hrumph. I don't always notice, but occasionally I do. I want to stare back and have tried it a few times but feel too embarrassed to do so, which is odd because the people doing it to me are guilty of utter rudeness.

What makes us so intriguing that we elicit these looks? Do we cause interest due to the differences in our age or the colour of our skin? Do we cause offence and question people's beliefs? Obviously, for some, the idea of a woman being with a younger man is still taboo, as is the idea of marrying someone from another ethnic background. There is no escaping the fact that I am older than Conrad, but when we see ourselves in the mirror or in photographs, or when friends see us, all we see are just Lis and Conrad.

Despite the looks, we've never had any racist comments from strangers when we've been out together. Conrad has never been stopped under the 'stop and search' law when he drove in London or Birmingham. Any negative comments we have received have been from people I know, or we met at social occasions. Plus, of course our closest relatives: our mothers, neither of whom were happy initially. In the year before she died, Mum had come to realise what a lovely, caring person Conrad is. In my eyes it took her way too long, especially when most of her friends had come to this decision when they first met him.

We got mixed messages from Cynthia too. While visiting her in London, she told me, "I'm glad he has found someone responsible".

Then, a few minutes later in the kitchen, she asked Conrad, "Why are you with her?"

My mum continued her off-the-cuff comments that would have been racist had they not been so funny. She once rang me to tell me to watch TV because, "Conrad's people were on the news." It was the Notting Hill Carnival. *Yes, Mum, he is related to every one of them!*

While staying with us for Christmas she was watching the Queens' Speech, and we were both in the kitchen washing up after the meal. I took her a cup of tea and, because as far as she was concerned we were disrespecting the Queen by not watching, she had the nerve to say "Hmmm! If it wasn't for the Queen, people like Conrad wouldn't be here."

I was so angry I snapped back, "And if you hadn't invited them here after the war, you wouldn't have had the help you needed."

Slamming the door, I went back into the kitchen where Conrad calmed me down. He was far more forgiving of Mum's thoughtless outbursts than I was.

Most comments we received however were just plain insensitive. My Godmother's comment "Well, if you have a couple of years, that will be good," was more about our age difference. She followed it with, "Relationships don't last long with people you meet in clubs." She had *obviously* had experience.

A businessman who I met while networking, when he saw a photo of Conrad on my phone, assumed, "I thought you'd be married to a white, middle-class man."

At a party, a Caribbean girl, who neither of us knew, but was also a guest and had been talking to us, confronted Conrad when I went to get a drink with: "Why aren't you with a sister?" He was so surprised, he didn't reply.

A long-term, white, male friend of mine made the most typical racial assumption. He offered to show me that a white man could be as good in bed as a black man. I declined his generous offer and he quickly went down in my estimation.

Some of our friends have been nervous that their children might say something about Conrad's colour. Children are naturally inclined to ask questions about the world around them and do so with innocence. Asha, our previous young neighbour, always used to climb onto a seat so she was tall enough to see over the fence and talk to him when he was in the garden.

One day she asked him, "Why is your skin so dark?"

Standing next to her, her mum grimaced.

Conrad was thinking of an answer, when I replied, "Because his mummy has the same coloured skin, and God makes people with all different shades of skin."

Asha seemed happy with this and was quiet for a while.

Then she said to Conrad, "You've got a big nose."

We couldn't stop laughing, but her mum was mortified. She had always been worried about Asha saying something that embarrassed her.

Conrad regularly gets asked, "Where are you from?"

When he answers he is born here, they say, "No, where are you from originally?"

If in the first place they asked him, "Where are your family from?" they would find out his ethnic origin. When speaking to someone who is from another culture, I sometimes ask them where they from, and then if they answer they were born here, I ask the latter question. There's nothing wrong with asking questions if you are genuinely interested in the person. Most people are only too happy to tell you.

It seems to me that many white, British people are worried they are going to use the wrong words and give offence. I know that when I was young I was very worried about inadvertently saying something discourteous to people, because I might use the incorrect language. Nowadays, it is made harder due to political correctness. Words used to describe people who aren't Caucasian change regularly and what may have been acceptable a few years ago is no longer correct. However, I'm not excusing racists, but those of the population who don't know many people outside of their community and are genuinely confused as to what words they should use.

As a couple we find it sad that, even now, decades after the mass immigration of people from Commonwealth countries to help us after the Second

World War, we continue to talk about the 'first black member of parliament' or the 'first Asian judge'.

There is a perceived immigration problem at the moment, due to the sheer numbers of people coming into the country. However, we are no longer purely 'white', and we haven't been for generations. We have a history over the centuries of people from many ethnicities who have helped build our country to where we are today. We are all British.

My parents were the type of people who lived their lives in a bubble, expecting everyone else to live the same way. They watched events on TV or read about them in the newspaper, but they didn't experience it themselves. Despite Dad working in the largest area in Leicester populated by an Asian community at the time, he knew no one from that group, and I doubt he ever interacted in any depth with anyone either. As you grow you either want to explore, or you stay the same. Neither of my parents wanted to travel further afield and see the world. They existed in their small world. I'm forever grateful they allowed me the opportunity to travel outside of mine.

We are by no means unique, apart from who we are as individuals. Conrad's and my story is merely a view into our life, and we know there are people out there who have to endure far worse situations than we ever have had to face.

There are many couples out there who have married from different racial backgrounds, but still in the 21st century the two of us being together can raise eyebrows. A relationship between mixed ethnic groups and also couples where the woman is older is becoming more common.

As a teenager I loved the song *Melting Pot* by Blue Mink. It talked about, (in what are now non-pc lyrics) the world being a melting pot of cultures and ethnicities. In what was perhaps my naivety, this was what my ideal world looked like. I didn't go out to find people from another culture and as you have read my life has been pretty socially narrow, but I have always been open to ideas and beliefs.

When I met Conrad, I wasn't thinking about his ethnicity. Initially I was attracted to his good looks and beautiful eyes and smile, and as I got to know him more, his wonderful personality. All of the things that make up his being are what I love, and the colour of his skin is part of him, as is mine. It's not nationality or colour of skin – it's the core values that we share.

On paper, we shouldn't have anything in common, when you consider the difference in our ages, backgrounds, education, and experiences, but the main thing is, we love each other deeply and have found our soul mate in each other.

I've always been a scaredy-cat when it comes to physical things. As a child, I would never have accepted a dare and as I've got older I've become more nervous of doing things outside my physical comfort zone, especially sport. However, I'm not scared of taking risks with my life in terms of trying new ideas and ventures.

Conrad, on the other hand, is willing to try anything physical and throws himself into adventures. He also likes trying new ideas and ventures. Both of us love meeting new people and have developed friendships with people from different cultures around the world.

Like any other relationship that works, we put time and effort into working at ours, and endeavour not to take each other for granted. We give each other time. We support each other's ideas and dreams, and never, ever belittle or embarrass each other in front of others. Over the years we have built our own traditions for Christmas and other holiday periods. Alongside our love of films, the most important part of our life is music. We laugh every day. We always hold hands before going to sleep. And, together, we enjoy the adventure that life brings.

Lightning Source UK Ltd.
Milton Keynes UK
UKHW01f0242081018
330070UK00003B/65/P